The Ascension Dimension

Transformational Keys for Spiritual Ascension

The Teachings of Sanat Kumara

Other Offerings by Terri Love

1. To be released in 2008:
   "The Ascension Dimension Oracle Cards"

2. To be released in 2008:
   "The Ascension Dimension Portal"

3. Terri Love's Guided Meditation CD's:
   - Inner Peace
   - Chakra Balance
   - Abundant Success
   - Healing Body, Mind & Spirit
   - Abundant Joy, Co-Creating with Angels
   - Your Past Lives
   - Heavenly Dreams for Children
   - Embrace Your Shadows
   - Sleepytime
   - Heavenly Relaxation
   - Smoking Cessation
   - Permanent Weight Reduction
   - Permanent Weight Reduction, Continued

4. Private Dialoged Sessions with Sanat Kumara
   For more information, visit *www.terrilove.com*

5. Dialoged Group Sessions with Sanat Kumara
   For more information, visit *www.terrilove.com*

6. Please visit *www.terrilove.com* for a full listing
   of Terri's private and group sessions for Hypno-
   therapy and the Emotional Freedom Technique.

The
Ascension Dimension
Transformational Keys for Spiritual Ascension

The Teachings of Sanat Kumara
Dialoged by Terri Love

Ancient Wisdom Publishing
Peoria, Arizona

Cover Artist; Ewa Niemczynska;
Email, *ewaniemczynska@yahoo.com*
Cover photograph copyright ©2008, Ancient Wisdom Publishing

Ancient Wisdom Publishing
P.O. Box 5635
Peoria, Arizona 85385

For all book orders, please email Terri C. Love or order directly from website.
terrilove@cox.net
www.terrilove.com

Library of Congress Control Number – 2008901084

Love, Terri C.
    The Ascension Dimension/by Terri Charlene Love
    p. 224 cm. 21
    ISBN 978-0-9814661-3-2
    1. Spiritual, Self-Help-United States. I. Title

Foreword

by Terri Love

Sanat has asked me to share, what it has meant to me to work with Him. As long as I can remember, God has been an integral part of my existence. I chose the Southern Baptist experience as a child and at age 18, I read a book about Beloved Buddha, at that time, my journey of remembering All that God Is, began.

My metaphysical journey of spiritual enlightenment has always included the Royal Angelic Realm and Nature Family in everyday experience. In January 2006, Sanat Kumara came into my meditation and asked me if He could use my vocal cords to manifest God's Will on Beloved Terra.

I spent three months, making sure this was God's Will for me, and in April of 2006, I did my first group dialog with Sanat Kumara. From that moment, I have not ceased to be amazed at the depth of Love, Sanat Kumara shares through me for all who listen. He is concerned first and foremost with the Highest Good of each individual and truly delivers what they 'need' to hear on a SOUL Level. His joyful, sense of humor is always respectful and filled with Love. He cares naught about 'proof', and challenges the individual to look within and find their answers, always reminding us of 'Faith'.

The God I Love is THE Creator that Sanat Kumara Loves.

I serve Mother/Father God from a space of humble Joy, and Sanat Kumara has added the Ascension Dimension to my life. He continues to guide me daily in manifesting God's Will. Each day, I awaken with my Angels and SK and eagerly look forward to what will unfold.

It is my sincere desire that as you read this, your Heart will open to the amazing potential of manifesting God's Will, if you would ask the Ascended Masters to come into your life. Sanat Kumara is One among Many Ascended Masters, ask within your Heart and you will not be disappointed. God will bring into your life the Ascended Master that is for your Highest Good. And from that space you will be greatly amazed and delighted as you open to the Divine Vibration of the Ascension Dimension.

My spiritual journey has been on the 'fast track', which would not have happened had I not listened to my Heart and allowed Sanat Kumara to guide me. I am forever grateful and appreciative to Sanat Kumara, Angels, Nature and Mother/Father God and all those who hold the vigil for Right-use-ness, Love and Joy in this amazing journey on Beloved Terra

Thank you for allowing me to share from my Heart.

Terri Charlene Love

Table of Contents

Introduction

Sanat Kumara heralds the Golden Age of Enlightenment, bringing in the Ascension Dimension on Beloved Terra.

"That which is not seen is more real and powerful than what is seen with the human eye. Learn to see through the Illusion." Sanat Kumara

Ascended Master, Sanat Kumara is known as the Ancient of Days.

He steps forward, now, from the Spiritual Hierarchy, dialoging through Terri Love, to share His Teachings.

"THE ASCENSION DIMENSION" is Sanat's, Do-It-Yourself, practical guide for the serious spiritual student.

Sanat Kumara brings treasures to Light, answering questions about Life, Liberty and the Pursuit of Happiness. His ability to enlighten and heal with Love will bring joy to your journey and hope to your Heart, stirring within a longing to remember, All That You Are.

He asks that you come with Sincerity in your Heart and He WILL Assist You.

Sanat Kumara combines His Ascended Vibration with the Royal Angelic Realm, Nature Family and the Spiritual Hierarchy for the Highest Good on Mother Earth and shares treasures of Love and Light for the readers of this book.

Sanat Kumara Asks You These Pertinent Spiritual Questions?

1. Is there a better way, to go about my business?

2. Am I crossing my 't's and dotting my 'i's?

3. Is my life filled with Quality?

4. Am I stuck?

5. Am I allowing Unconditional Love?

6. Am I investing in my Spiritual Bank?

7. Is FAITH a key component in my priorities?

8. Am I Qualifying my Energy with Life?

9. Am I moving from a space of non-judgment?

10. Am I asking God to guide me?

11. Is God's Will a top priority in my life?

12. Am I feeding my SOUL?

Part One

"THE ASCENSION DIMENSION"
Transformational Keys for Spiritual Ascension

SACRED FIRE

I AM SACRED FIRE, HOLY TRINITY
HEART OF MOTHER/FATHER GOD
DIVINE WILL, JOY, AND LOVE, IN LIBERTY

The Teachings of SANAT KUMARA

I AM Beloved Sanat Kumara and I have chosen to share spiritual inspiration for healing on all levels. This information is given from My Heart for those who are willing to look within and receive into their Hearts. I dialog through Terri with the Master Number 33, which vibrates as Master of Healing Energies through Love. Love IS the greatest force upon Mother Earth and it is this Unconditional Love that will heal your Heart Space and manifest your Highest Good. I AM from the Planet Venus and my Twin Flame is Beloved Lady Venus. We have created Shamballa, an Etheric temple over the Gobi Desert. Shamballa holds the Holographic Pattern of your Electronic Presence and as each individual continues to connect with their Electronic Presence, Shamballa will manifest in the physical realm. The road to Shamballa is creating

Heaven on Earth, and I come forth now to anchor the Will of Mother/Father God, glorifying the Divine Plan set forth into motion before time began.

To the reader: I wish for you to understand, My Ascended Vibration will be with you as you move through this book. I share with the intention of giving Hope, for those who will be open to explore that which comes for them as a result of reading My information. It is not by mistake that this book is in your hands, and I will assist you, on a SOUL Level to embrace your Destiny and manifest that which is for your Highest Good. Each time you read these pages, please call on Me, and I will help you to open up your Heart, as you have never been able to do so before now, and that very action, will manifest Heaven within you.

It is Written. So Be It and So It Is.

"A soft breeze filters through your mind and you remember a time from long ago, a memory that stirs within your Heart Space. And that remembering is Now as you come to recognize your True Nature goes beyond the physical, yes, your Cosmic Beingness goes beyond time and space. And as you remember this stirring within your Heart, it calls forth a yearning of that part of you which is One with All That Is, I AM THAT I AM. This is your Diamond Core God Cell, SACRED FIRE, calling forth for you to stand up and BE, I AM, all that you are destined to be.

It is your **Destiny** to fulfill your Divine Blueprint, and to deny it is to deny the very air that you breathe. You cannot deny this part of you (I AM) that is Eternal, for in this Eternal Space you are One with that which created you, Mother/Father God. Divine Blueprint calls to you, and as you move forward through these pages, I, Beloved Sanat Kumara will speak truths from the Heart of Mother/Father God that will set you free. For I will speak to you of that which you have forgotten and Now, are ready to remember.

And I say to you, remember, that which is not seen is more real and powerful than that which is seen with the human eye. Learn to see through the ***Illusion AND FLOW IN THE ASCENSION DIMENSION!!!***

DIVINE BLUEPRINT STEP FORWARD
DIVINE BLUEPRINT STEP FORWARD
DIVINE BLUEPRINT STEP FORWARD and BE, [I AM].

The First Key

SOUL

There is a most precious space that has become recognized through out the Universe, yes, even through out all Galaxies as the place that holds the Infinite Mind of Mother/Father God. This Holy Space is known as SOUL. SOUL is God's perfect creation. In fact, SOUL is the only creation throughout the Universe, which holds LIFE.

And within this Holy Space, God placed the SACRED FIRE manifested as the Heart of SOUL.

It is this place called **SACRED FIRE**, that burns eternal in your Heart, where the Three Fold Flame holds your Divine Blueprint. Divine Blueprint is the Map of your Electronic Presence. Your Diamond Core God Cell is within this Holy Altar. You, My Beloved Sisters and Brothers of the Light have served at this Holy Altar in many time/space realities.

For your SOUL is Eternal, and SOUL not only understands the Divine Vibration of Mother/Father God, SOUL yearns to create fully and completely that which complements your Divinity.

Anything that comes from a vibration (less than) LOVE is the *Illusion* which robs your consciousness of Mother/Father God Blessings.

It is this special unique vibration, your *Divine Vibration,* that SOUL nudges you to manifest, daily, hourly, minute by minute, second by second.

You hold a most unique vibration that no one before you or after you will ever vibrate. It is your destiny, to add this most precious *Divine Vibration* to the Collective Consciousness. Mother/Father God is counting on you, My Beloved Friends, to fulfill your Destiny, and add your very special *Divine Vibration.*

Through countless lifetimes, SOUL has nurtured you, SOUL has embraced you, yes SOUL has sat with you and encouraged you to explore, experiment and create. SOUL is your Divine Essence. *SOUL is your Divine Birthing Place.* SOUL is who and what you are and SOUL has the Multi-Dimensional Ability to create from several different aspects, levels and realms all at the same time. This is the beauty of SOUL.

SOUL is THE prototype of Mother/Father God and SOUL has been evolving from the beginning of its Creation. SOUL yearns to navigate with Divine Vibration, creating experiences that escalate the Joy, Love and Light of Mother/Father God.

SOUL chooses to expand the Essence of Love and Light, in new and grander avenues of awareness. Which is where you come in!! Your experience becomes a virtual playground for unlimited possibilities and always, always, always there is a *Divine Vibration.*

SOUL is what you have come from and SOUL is what you are returning to.

This is the Beauty of your Heart Space (which I will expand on in Chapter 3, Heart of Sacred Fire).

It is here within your Heart Space, your Divine Blueprint is encoded with your unique *Divine Vibration.* (I will discuss Divine Vibration in greater detail in Chapter 4.)

Mother/Father God created many SOULS, each having what is known as a SOUL Group. Your SOUL is represented by a Council of Twelve, "I AM" Presences, also known as Monads.

These Twelve, "I AM" Presences each have a Twin Flame, Male/Female Essence, perfectly balanced and harmonized in the Love and Light of Mother/Father God. And each of the 'I AM' Presences, journeyed out as male/female expressions.

SOUL Groups have various expressions, some incarnated (which covers many galaxies and not all human), some in spirit form, and some in the Ascended State.

All SOUL Groups are from the Beginning of Creation, some have evolved at a quicker pace, please remember there is no judgment, just experience with Mother/Father God.

I will share with you a glorious truth that will assist you in moving through 3D Illusion.

At any given moment throughout your day, call your SOUL Group Energy in to surround you. (Get into the habit, of ***imagining color*** when you proceed spiritually, I will explain this further in Chapter 13, Energy)

Your SOUL Group carries a most glorious combination of spiritually enlightened frequencies, the Divine Vibration of Ascended Cosmic Beings, which will provide valuable assistance in any situation.

The Kingdom's of Ascended Masters. Angels, Nature, and Galactic Light Beings comprise your SOUL Group Energy.

Your SOUL Group is available to you, just through your thought!! Call upon your SOUL Group, you WILL move forward in the Love & Light of Mother/Father God in monumental leaps and bounds.

Now, from SOUL, each Twin Flame has separated and journeyed, through vast multi-dimensional experiences. Your Twin Flame is your Divine Complement. Your Twin Flame is to you what Yin and Yang are in Energy. It is that part of you which completes you in Divine Vibration.

You each separated from 'I AM' to express in male, female energies that which is for the Highest Good of SOUL. And those expressions have created many experiences to glorify the Love & Light of Mother/Father God.

There may be a space where the Male Energy of the 'I AM' Presence, makes the Ascension and the Female Energy of the 'I AM' Presence remains in the un-ascended state.

Eventually, My Dear Friends, you will come to the space of returning to your Twin Flame in the Glory of Divine Alignment within 'I AM', Mother/Father God. And this re-uniting is your destiny.

It IS the Will of Mother/Father God that all 'I AM' Presences, become One with Divine Mind, in the Ascended State.

And from SOUL, the Angelic Realm and Nature Family (which includes the Animal Kingdom) have evolved.

These vast and glorious expressions make up your SOUL Group. All have expressed and experienced in various forms of Energy, because you said you would take the **Divine Vibration** of Mother/Father God and expand it, ever increasing the Love & Light of All That Is.

You said you would assist SOUL to build a strong foundation for Divine Mind to expand. And always there is a vibration.

And it IS this **Divine Vibration** of SOUL that is a most valuable key to Spiritual Ascension.

You have come from SOUL, and SOUL was created

by Mother/Father God.

You chose to participate in this playground on Mother Earth. The reasons are as varied as the life forms on your planet, and it is an amazingly grand scheme of things happening here and now on Beloved Terra.

And the most important question the student of Spiritual Ascension needs to ask themselves, "Am I feeding my Soul?"

DIVINE BLUEPRINT STEP FORWARD
DIVINE BLUEPRINT STEP FORWARD
DIVINE BLUEPRINT STEP FORWARD and BE [I AM].

The Second Key

SPIRITUAL ASCENSION

Spiritual Ascension is the ability to move through all dimensions in your Light Body, your Merkabah, and eventually re-unite with your Twin Flame, your *I AM PRESENCE, I AM THAT I AM,* with all of the glorious Divine Vibrations of experience that you have gathered.

And may I add here, there is no Be-All, End-All finish to this marvelous journey called LIFE. It is ongoing, always expanding and the JOY of expressing Love & Light is a continuous process that goes on through Infinity.

Remember, my Brothers and Sisters, Spiritual Ascension happens on many levels.

And for you who chose to participate in the 3rd dimension of *Illusion,* Spiritual Ascension is most assuredly a grand thing to move towards; for Spiritual Ascension from 3D moves one into 5D, where you move beyond the birth and death cycle.

In the 5th dimension you have earned the privilege to express your Light Body, balanced in the Love & Light of Mother/Father God.

Please understand, the 3rd dimension afforded you grand opportunities to experience the nature of duality, yin and yang, negative and positive.

This 3D *Illusion* has become an experiment that will go down in History to afford one of the most *Exclusive Vibrations* ever to come from Divine Mind.

Because of this 3D *Illusion* experiment, you have been able to escalate your consciousness faster than ever before, no where else has this been possible throughout the Universe.

It is a world of gratitude, We of the Spiritual Hierarchy, give to Mother Earth.

And because Beloved Terra has given so unselfishly of Her Energy, more SOUL groups have evolved such glorious Divine Vibrations for the Heavens to behold, that Earth will be known throughout the Universe as the School for the Gods. And so Beloved Terra will shine in the Heavens as none before Her. It is written, So Be It & So It Is.

Are you going to be a part of this, My Dear Friends?

Spiritual Ascension is your most glorious journey of evolving and enlightenment on a multi-dimensional ladder.

It is SOUL Co-Creating with Mother/Father God as 'I AM' into Infinity. [I AM] vibrates the numerological value of five, which is FREEDOM.

Think on this for a moment. Ask yourself these questions.

- ***What does Freedom mean to me at this time in my life?***

- ***How long do I keep repeating the old patterns that do not support LIFE?***

- ***How long do I continue down the path that fails to fulfill my passions?***

- ***When do I stop and make the decision that enough is enough?***

- ***At what point do I learn to take responsibility for my Energy?***

These are pertinent questions that all spiritual students *must* ask themselves?

I AM Sanat Kumara, and I too came to a place within My journey, and I had to take a long, penetrating look within Myself and make decisions. It was those decisions which I now share with you in this book.

Each individual life form must recognize, you are either Master of Energy or Energy is Master of you. No exceptions. It is the Law!!

Sooner or later, everyone will come to a place where they decide which road they are going to travel. When opportunity knocks, one has a choice. And choice always carries a vibration. And with that vibration, there are multitudes of expression for each to participate in.

Ideally, the individual realizes there is a vibration within their life that is lacking. Here, the life form recognizes a yearning to know (reconnect with) that which created it. And it is in this recognition; the individual learns to follow their HEART.

AND IT IS WITHIN THE **HEART OF SACRED FIRE** THAT ALL ANSWERS EXIST. NO EXCEPTION. This is how Mother/Father God intended it to be.

Throughout this book, I will continuously bring your awareness to 'Heart of Sacred Fire'. *Your journey began in your Heart of Sacred Fire a long time ago. And it is within this SACRED FIRE that you will return home to All That You Are.*

I AM SANAT KUMARA, AND I STATE TO THE UNIVERSE, YOUR HEART OF SACRED

**FIRE HOLDS ALL THE KEYS TO YOUR SPIRI-
TUAL ASCENSION. IT IS WITHIN THE SACRED
FIRE THAT YOU WILL LEARN TO BE STILL,
AND KNOW 'I AM'.**
It is written. So Be It and So It Is.

Spiritual Ascension can become taxing at the
physical level. Please understand, there is no right
way or wrong way to evolve, rather it becomes your
journey of **LETTING GO** of the old paradigms, the old
programs, healing on all levels and knowing the AT-
ONE-MENT of Mother/Father God.

*The key is don't get stuck. If you notice a stuck
energy within you, remove it!! And if you don't
know how, keep reading this book. I will show you
how to LET GO of stuck energy, just ask Me!!*

As you proceed forward in your evolutionary journey, you may notice moments of physical exhaustion,
get the needed rest that your body is telling you it
needs. Sleep is by far one of the most beneficial
avenues that you can give to your physical body. It is
in the sleep state, that your physical body repairs and
you connect with your SOUL Group, your Angels, your
Spirit Guides and your Higher Self. You are truly very
busy in the sleep state and yet this is a most beneficial
time for you on all levels. So give your physical body
the sleep it is telling you that it needs.

You may also recognize, when you wake up that
you feel you are not quite able to connect with your
body, even though you know you ARE in your physical
body. I can hear some of you saying right now, yes
Sanat, I have felt that so many times.

I am sharing this with you for clarification of experience as you move from 3D to 5D.

Your Entire Being is literally being re-wired for 5D, and your physical body is trying to catch up.

It may even seem as if you have experienced a physical death!!

Not to worry, just be aware of your body's physical needs, and understand this WILL pass.

There may be moments of mental exhaustion, which feels as if you are depressed, blah, lack of confidence, questioning your self-worth, and loneliness. *Please remember, these are signs of the Lower Ego letting go and you are letting go of all the stuck energies that have held you back (AKA the Illusion)!!*

This too shall pass, call on my Ascended Vibration to assist you through this, memorize the Heart of Sacred Fire Meditation and these Spiritual Ascension Keys.

These Ascended Vibration Tools will greatly assist you to move through the Illusion and to enjoy the Love & Light of Mother/Father God Energy.

(And here I will add, as I AM taking the time to point these things out for you, please recognize the importance of following through with these suggestions!!)

You would do yourself much good to watch what you are eating and drinking, recognizing that nutritional value will give you the fuel you need to get the job done!!

Call on your Angels, they will gladly assist you in fueling your body with the correct nutrition, just ask them. I will also guide you, please ask Me.

You will learn to listen to your **Heart of Sacred Fire**. *The journey of Spiritual Ascension requires your Undivided Attention.* Think about this for just a moment. Your undivided attention, what does this mean to you?

If your attention is on everything that is not right in your life, your attention is scattered.

What is amiss in your life has come to teach you and I will discuss this in detail in Chapter 16, Higher Self.

At any given moment throughout your day, ask yourself, is my attention divided, scattered? You have heard the old saying "A house divided against itself, cannot stand".

This refers to consciousness. If your Heart is telling you one thing and your mind is telling you another, you will remain divided. Which is another way of stating, you are stuck, and now you are beginning to recognize the *Illusion!!*

And I would like to add here, your Mind carries your conscious factor, your Heart carries your subconscious factor.

If your attention is scattered, your attention is divided. Here you recognize 'stuck'!!

    ✍ **PRACTICE UNDIVIDED ATTENTON.**
    ✍ **PRACTICE UNDIVIDED ATTENTION.**
    ✍ **PRACTICE UNDIVIDED ATTENTION.**

How does one do this? As you proceed through your day, you will become familiar with your **Heart of Sacred Fire.** This is that *Holy Space* within your Heart Chakra. It is in the **SACRED FIRE** that you will learn to **REST** in the **NOW & BE,** and as you proceed through these pages, My Ascended Vibration will enable you to understand this information from a Divine Vantage Point.

    ✍ *Learn to Set with DIVINE INTENTION, as you REST in the NOW*

- *DIVINE INTENTION will bring NOW to you*
- *Your Undivided Attention comes through Divine Intention = NOW*
- *Create God's Will NOW, in your Life & Flow in the Ascension Dimension*
- *And REST, BE in your HEART OF SACRED FIRE*

My Dear Friends, the Journey of Spiritual Ascension is NOW, for NOW is all that there is. Everything else is the ILLUSION. Please remember, that which is not seen is more real and powerful than that which is seen with the human eye. And this is precisely where one learns to be in tune with the Universe!!

SOUL calls you, SOUL nudges you and SOUL understands what needs to transpire for you to recognize the Divine Vibration of Spiritual Ascension. And as you move towards your Spiritual Ascension, you earn the right to become Co-Creators with Mother/Father God.

Vibration is in everything that you create and you will come to a space in your life when you recognize your vibration is either moving you forward or keeping you stuck!

When you understand this, you will learn to recognize Divine Vibration is one of the Transformational Keys to Higher Consciousness and your Spiritual Ascension.

There is a synergistic effect with vibration which creates a playground for feelings.

And when you create with the Divine Vibration of Love, Light, Joy, Respect, Freedom and Gratitude, you are flowing with Divine Mind and practicing being in tune with the Universe.

This moves you away from the Illusion of 3D, manifesting 5D in your Heart of Sacred Fire.

DIVINE BLUEPRINT STEP FORWARD
DIVINE BLUEPRINT STEP FORWARD
DIVINE BLUEPRINT STEP FORWARD and BE, [I AM]

HEART OF SACRED FIRE

And so, this Holy Space known as **'Sacred Fire',** it is in your Heart. Beloved Archangel Michael and His Twin flame Archeia Faith, it is Their sacred honor as Keepers of the Threefold flame within your Heart Space, (no matter what may come) to fan it and keep the Holy Altar sacred, as Mother/Father God intended.

It has become a common misconception throughout mankind's journey that your 'mind' must make important decisions for you, based upon facts and figures, etc.

I AM Sanat Kumara, and now share truths that will set you free from the *Illusion.*

Your 'mind' can be a very special tool for moving through the 3D experience. And yet, the serious student of Spiritual Ascension will learn to recognize that 'human mind' is seated in the lower dimensional vibrations, unable to grasp concepts of *'that which cannot be seen with the human eye'.*

Mind in and of itself is beneficial for assisting the individual to gather knowledge, and humans have proven this to be a quest of great honor in many circles. Through trial and tribulation, mankind has experienced this thirst for knowledge, which has led many down empty roads filled with power, ego and futile attempts to control.

Mother/Father God has always had a most glorious plan in place and it is that plan that has led you to read this book.

Your Heart, My Dear Friends, holds the answers to LIFE. *Your Heart houses your Divine Blueprint, anchored within your Cosmic Beingness.*

There is no-thing, there is no event, there is no person, past, present or future that can take this away from you and it is called LIFE.

And again I say, "That which is not seen, is more powerful, than what is seen with the Human Eye. Learn to see beyond the Illusion".

Within your Heart, lie all your answers.

- Always, always, always, go to your Heart and *ask* for guidance and you WILL receive from Divine Mind.
- Always, always, always, go to your Heart and *listen,* and you WILL receive, directly from Divine Mind.
- Always, always, always, go to your Heart and *feel,* and you WILL receive from Divine Mind.

The 3-D *Illusion* has been one of duality, which you said you would participate in. Yes, duality came with a price.

Yin and Yang, Negative and Positive Polarities, allowed all of you to create with choice.

And participate you have, through innumerable applications, you have put to the test the *Illusion* of 3D.

And Oh, My Dear Friends, what a vast and amazing plethora of vibrations you have participated in.

'All' is a journey of vibration, and in that vibration you experience the depth and width and vastness of Source Energy.

Please remember, there is no judgment in Mother/Father God, only experience!! Mother/Father God does not look at LIFE as right or wrong, good or bad, just experience!

And still Mother/Father God, holds you in the purest form of Unconditional Love that honors you, nurtures you, motivates you to reunite with that which created you.

Here, I feel some ask the question, why did I leave the arms of Mother/Father God?

My Beloved, it has been from a Heart of purest Unconditional Love that SOUL allowed All to venture forth, and collectively add to Divine Consciousness.

Mother/Father God created SOUL and from SOUL came multitudes of life forms, all with a Divine Vibration.

This Divine Vibration yearns to co-create with Divine Mind from your own unique perception and vantage point, and it has led all of you on a most glorious journey we call LIFE.

Yes, My Beloved Friends, this experience we call LIFE is a most precious expression that Mother/Father God created. I would like to add here, there is no other experience in the entire Universe that equals LIFE.

And, I hear some asking how can Mother/Father God allow terrible things to occur on our Planet? And once again, I say, Free Will and Choice. Divine Mind allows Free Will and Choice and with this comes responsibility! And that is precisely why you are reading my book!! (I will discuss more on Free Will and Choice in Chapter 8)

LIFE comes from Mother/Father God and is absolutely, beyond compare, the most Holy Privilege ever given and it vibrates 'I AM'. AS

YOU MOVE TOWARDS THIS SPACE OF RECOG-NIZING THE PRIVILEGE THAT YOU HAVE BEEN GIVEN, YOU WILL REMEMBER ALL THAT YOU ARE, and you will come Home.

And the Royal Angelic Realm will sing praises to God for you!!!!!

It is written, So Be It and So It Is.

And you have come from SOUL to participate in this expression, known as LIFE, which I will expand on as we go.

All information, all memories, all maps, are housed within this most Sacred Space in your Hearts. No exceptions!

The game of *Illusion* on Beloved Terra is about to end, my Dear Friends, and please allow Me to clarify, this game of *Illusion* has been all about the Lower Ego, which is 3D. And We of the Spiritual Hierarchy have stepped forward NOW, to assist Mother Earth to raise the Collective Consciousness to the 5th Dimension.

It is NOW time, for all to listen to their Heart of Sacred Fire.

I AM SANAT KUMARA, AND I STATE TO THE UNIVERSE, YOUR HEART OF SACRED FIRE HOLDS ALL THE KEYS TO YOUR SPIRI-TUAL ASCENSION. IT IS WITHIN THE SACRED FIRE THAT YOU WILL LEARN TO BE STILL, AND KNOW 'I AM'.

It is written. So Be It and So It Is.

My Beloved Friends, I speak to you an Eternal Truth when I say, your Heart will not lie to you. As a matter of fact, you can take that to your Spiritual Bank and invest it!!

Think on this for a moment, your Heart tells you what is right for you. Your Heart tells you when it is time to let go. Your Heart tells you to rest, when there is nothing more that you can do at that moment. Your Heart always speaks to you, and yet you have spent numerous lifetimes not listening!!! Wake Up!!

Truly, My Dear Friends, your Heart has been waiting for you to listen for a long, long, time. You know when your Heart is speaking to you, it speaks quietly, and this is where that still, small voice comes from within you. Right there in your Heart! This is wisdom at its finest. Your Heart speaks to you, which is your God Presence, always for your Highest Good.

Your Heart has a Divine Agenda, because Divine Mind created your Heart and it will not allow you to forget.

That is why I, Beloved Sanat Kumara, AM here now, reminding you.

It is time, to get out of your heads, LET GO of the need to control, and follow your Hearts.
It is time, to get out of your heads, LET GO of the need to control, and follow your Hearts.
It is time, to get out of your heads, LET GO of the need to control, and follow your Hearts.

This is where your Inner Sanctuary rests. It has always been there, within your Heart of Sacred Fire, and it will ride the storm and carry you safely Home. Go within and rest (BE).

This resting (BE-ing) within your Heart of Sacred Fire takes practice. You learn to come with *sincerity* into your Inner Sanctuary. You learn to come with *gratitude,* and last but not least, you learn to come with *surrender.*

- These Sacred Vibrations of **Sincerity, Gratitude, and Surrender** open your Heart and allow Divine Mind to anchor God's Will and move you forward to fulfill your Destiny.
- It is here, that you learn to allow Higher Self (God Presence) to flow Heaven down through your Chakra System. (As Above, So Below)
- It is here that you learn to *let go* of the Lower Ego and **REST (BE).**
- It is here that you recognize, REST (BE) IS VITAL TO YOUR ASCENSION
- It is here within your Heart of Sacred Fire that you allow the Will of Mother/Father God, and manifest within the Ascension Dimension Cord.
- **And it is here that you learn to test all things.** You will learn to test if what you are hearing is from Lower Ego or your Higher Self (God Presence).
- *YOUR HEART WILL NOT LIE!!!!!!!!*

Here is the question to always ask yourself, and you will know by your answer if it is your Heart speaking:

If I follow through with this, will it give me Peace and Joy within my Heart?

Learn to ask yourself this question before you follow through and you **WILL** know if it comes from your Heart.

Always, always, always, go within your Heart and see how it feels!

If it is God, it will feel right, good and honorable for you. There is a forward momentum of Energy to honor LIFE. This is *'Qualifying LIFE'.*

If it is of the Lower Ego, it will feel depressing, sad and disrespectful to you. There is a lack of momentum, no honoring of LIFE. This is *'Mis-Qualifying Death'.*

This is a learning for everyone, it is a testing of a vibration, you learn to flow the Ascension Dimension Cord, between Heart and 3rd Eye and from there you manifest 'I AM', all with your Heart of Sacred Fire. I will explain this more as we go along.

All of your answers are within your Heart of Sacred Fire. No exceptions. Your Heart of Sacred Fire is the Divine Matrix (Replica) of your Electronic Presence.

And in that Divine Map, your SOUL Coding is woven with Divine Mind.

And with this information, comes everything you will ever need. Your **Heart of Sacred Fire** is your First Aid Kit, Your Do-It-Yourself, Self-Help Map for anything that comes up in this glorious journey!!

Please DO take that to your Spiritual Bank and invest it!!

Mother/Father God sent you equipped with the most advanced technology ever to be conceived within Divine Mind, and it is called HEART OF SACRED FIRE!!!

Your **Heart of Sacred Fire** has been one of the most overlooked treasures ever known and NOW is your opportunity to understand this information.

And you said, I will learn to Qualify Life from my **Heart of Sacred Fire!! (The Qualification of Energy is a natural power within your Heart, which flows the Ascension Dimension. Please memorize that statement as you continue through this book.)**

- *As you learn to REST (BE), you experience Atonement, AT-ONE-MENT.*
- *Atonement is a Holy Blending of all Dimensions within your Heart of Sacred Fire.*

    And as one experiences Atonement, one RESTS (BE) in surrender to Divine Mind, and it is in BE-ing, you are flowing Ascension Dimension.

    Practice A SURRENDER OF REST (BE-ing) AND YOU WILL KNOW the Ascension Dimension.

    I AM SACRED FIRE, HOLY TRINITY

In this sacred space of **Sincerity, Gratitude and Surrender** within your Heart, you will find a most glorious treasure house filled with more than you could ever possibly ask for or want. This is **ABUNDANT LIFE.**

It is a Divine Abode of Bliss and as you partake of this sacredness within your Heart, you heal all of the **Illusion.**

Yes, My Dear Friends, the **Illusion** has kept you in 3D, in a vibration of fear, lack, needy, wanting and struggle. Does this sound familiar?

Please remember, it is always a choice. And each circumstance avails you of an opportunity to choose with your free will. And now I hear you say, "I have a choice?"

"Oh Sanat, I did not choose that!!"

I say this in love, My Dear Friends, yes you did choose that, maybe not consciously; however, even if it was chosen on a SOUL Level, it is yours!! Step up to the plate, and take responsibility!!

You may stay in the Illusion of lack and fear, this is your journey and many have become familiar with the 'drama'. You know, 'been there, done that'!

When you have had enough of that, you will learn to test everything in your Heart of Sacred Fire. Remember, that which you resist, persists. When you surrender into your Heart of Sacred Fire with gratitude and sincerity, a song will fill your

Being with Divine Vibration for you will BE flowing the Ascension Dimension.

And now I will explain the 'test' from a Divine Vantage point of the Ascended Masters. And you **WILL** come out ahead of the game, as you learn to Rest (BE) in your Heart of Sacred Fire.

The Sacred Fire within your Heart holds every-thing you need to move forward in the Love and Light of Mother/Father God. And as you learn to move from your Heart Space, you learn to under-stand the Will of God, which is how you 'test'.

    THE WILL OF GOD ALWAYS QUALIFIES LIFE.
    THE WILL OF GOD ALWAYS QUALIFIES LIFE.
    THE WILL OF GOD ALWAYS QUALIFIES LIFE.

No exceptions. It is written. So Be It and So It Is.

And in this Divine Vibration of the Will of God, you recognize how to QUALIFY LIFE and Qualify Life from the Ascension Dimension Cord.

I will explain this more as we go along. **Your desires teach you how to Qualify Life and understand the Will of God, which flows the Ascension Dimension.** *Remember, the 'Qualification of Energy' is a natural power within your Heart of Sacred Fire, which flows the Ascension Dimension!!*

Many of you live in fear that God does not want you to see your desires fulfilled. That is the ***Illusion*** from Lower Ego. Mother/Father God always intended for your desires to lead you joyously in the Will of God, as you Qualify Life.

It all starts and stops within your Heart of Sacred Fire.

And in this recognition, you become Co-Creators with Mother/Father God, moving from your Heart of Sacred Fire, anchoring the Will of God within your Heart, and manifesting your desires from that Sacred Space. (I explain the Ascension Dimension Cord in My Heart of Sacred Fire Meditation.)

This, Beloved Friends, is sweet sincerity, gratitude and surrender, and IT IS the Unconditional Love of Divine Vibration.

And as you process this throughout your life, you embrace a *JOY* that can only come from moving in that space of Oneness with Mother/Father God Energy.

And that *JOY* becomes your motivation to experience more within your Heart Space.

And that *JOY* moves you to *PASSION,* and soon your *PASSION* leads you into the Arms of Mother/Father God Energy, Divine Vibration, and you realize you *have* returned Home.

My Beloved Friends, this is the reward that guides your Heart. That *feeling* of returning to, that which you have come from, a *sweet sincerity, gratitude and surrender.*

It is innately woven within your fabric and ultimately *will* lead you Home.

As the days go by, My Dear Friends, you will come to recognize your Heart Space is glowing and growing in strength. Light that resonates in your Heart will shine through your eyes for all to see and the day will come, that the Light and Love in your eyes will shine your path home, as you return to the Arms of Mother/Father God.

Hear Me now as I say to you, *Your Heart has a Mind of its own!! This has always been the Divine Plan from Divine Mind. Your Heart communicates information to each and every cell within your physical body. And with this information, Mother/ Father God intended each life stream, the full advantage of Divine Potential on a cellular level.*

Any information that is not in accordance with Divine Potential is the Illusion, allowed at some point for the benefit of recognizing a vibration other than Divine Vibration.

Your Cells contain information from ALL life experiences, as well as SOUL Group Collective Consciousness, and yet, your Cells also contain Divine Potential.

Please remember, All is allowed for the benefit of LIFE evolving in Love and Light.

This most honored place within your Heart holds the Matrix of your Electronic Light Body known in the Ancient Days as the Adam Kadmon Light Body.

This Matrix becomes activated each second you vibrate Unconditional Love and Light, Divine Vibration; AND the more you activate your Divine Essence, I AM THAT I AM, flows the Ascension Dimension. And so, the journey continues!!!!

DIVINE BLUEPRINT STEP FORWARD
DIVINE BLUEPRINT STEP FORWARD
DIVINE BLUEPRINT STEP FORWARD and BE, [I AM]

The Fourth Key

DIVINE VIBRATION

You have heard me refer to Divine Vibration. Vibration is the Energy that Universal Consciousness responds to. *This is a great truth that has been hidden from mankind for a long time on Beloved Mother Earth.* It has made the game of Duality very interesting, to say the least.

Hear this again, Universal Consciousness responds to vibration!

NO MATTER WHAT, Universal Consciousness responds to vibration!! And the Universe is always listening!!!

With that information, your frequency, your energy, your vibration is creating a Causal Body. It is this Causal Body that has been with you, since you began this journey of separation. Your Causal Body is Mother/Father God's gift to you.

It is the accumulation of Divine Vibration for all the good you have manifested. And for those of you, whom I hear right now, saying, 'I don't think I have done enough good".

Again, I remind you, that is the **ILLUSION!!**

That which is not seen, is more real and powerful than what is seen with the Human Eye. Learn to see through the *Illusion!*

Your Causal Body is God's promise to you of Heaven. And within your Causal Body, Divine Vibration is manifested each moment that you allow (receive, BE) I AM.

Divine Vibration is the frequency of the Ascension Dimension.
Divine Vibration is the frequency of the Ascension Dimension.
Divine Vibration is the frequency of the Ascension Dimension.

Now separation is neither good, nor bad, just an experience, that provided the **Illusion.** And because of this **Illusion** of separation, you have been experiencing different vibrations through countless lifetimes, and all of these vibrations have created a Causal Body.

Causal Body is holding all of the most glorious vibrations of Love and Light, for Causal Body is God's gift to you of Heaven on all levels, in all dimensions.

And it is this Causal Body that Mother/Father God wishes for you to enjoy the Divine Vibrations of all the good that you have done. Your Causal Body holds the Divine Vibration of righteousness, (right-use) of Life that has been Qualified with the Light and Love of Mother/Father God.

Any vibration that is of a lesser frequency has been transmuted by the Holy Spirit. Your Causal Body is God's Gift to you and your SOUL Group has a combined Causal Body from which you may utilize, according to your Highest Good!

Causal Body is your treasure chest. It holds all of the LIFE you have Qualified.

It is time, my Brothers and Sisters, to access your treasure chest, and all the Bells and Whistles that go with it!! The Spiritual Hierarchy is here to assist you. You have Qualified Life and you have Qualified Life in an Abundant Manner. Any information to the contrary is a lie!!

***You are worthy of Goodness, Honor,
Respect, Love and Light and all you have to
do is allow (receive) I AM!!***

I AM Sanat Kumara and I'm here to tell you now,
there are vast treasures of Heaven stored up for you in
your Causal Body and it is your Divine Heritage to
enjoy this abundant abode of bliss.

There are Divine Vibrations of glorious frequencies that sing praises to the Love & Light of
Mother/Father God and these same frequencies con-
stitute the Divine Fabric that house Causal Body.

Can you not see this picture I am creating for you?
Can you but for a moment, feel this Divine Vibration
that Mother/Father God, created in this glorious space
(Causal Body) for the outpouring of your Love, your
Sincerity, your Gratitude?

- Each time you allow thankfulness to well up
  inside of your Heart of Sacred Fire, you
  increase Divine Vibration.
- Each time you feel love and adoration flow
  from your Being to that which has created
  you, you increase Divine Vibration.
- Each time you choose appreciation with a
  frequency of gratitude, you increase
  Divine Vibration.

***This is Qualified Life, My Dear Brothers and
Sisters. This is what Heaven is made up of, Divine
Vibration and it holds treasures upon treasures for
you and it IS the Divine Plan of Mother/Father God for
you to express Heaven within your physical vehicle.***

***CAUSAL BODY IS TO YOUR SPIRITUAL ASCEN-
SION, what sunshine is to the life of a plant. That***

plant will not reach its fullest potential without the correct Light.

And your Spiritual Ascension will escalate each time you feed on the Divine Vibration stored up in your treasure chest, Causal Body. And you do this by allowing (receiving, BE-ing) I AM, within your HEART OF SACRED FIRE. The beauty of this is the more you feed on Divine Vibration in your Causal Body, the more your Divine Vibration expands in Causal Body. THIS IS THE SPIRITUAL ASPECT OF THE LAW OF ATTRACTION. As you practice Qualifying LIFE (which is your experience of NOW) within your Heart, you will access your Treasure Chest or Causal Body. Try it, you'll like it!!!

Set the Divine Intention, align with Causal Body and BE, I AM, in your Heart of Sacred Fire.

Meditate on these words and you WILL escalate up that evolutionary ladder towards your FREEDOM, flowing the Ascension Dimension.

Beloved Friends, do you find throughout your day that you become weary? Please remember, that I, Sanat Kumara, worked through the 3rd dimensional **Illusion** of fear, poverty, lust and conditional love. Everything that you go through, I understand, for I have experienced it also, as all Ascended Masters have who have chosen Spiritual Ascension.

Energy is the substance of Consciousness. (I will cover this more in Chapter 13, Energy.)

And it becomes your responsibility to Qualify Energy every second, for each second is filled with opportunities to flow in the Ascension Dimension.

Please remember: You are either Master of Energy, or Energy is Master of You.

Without exception, each life form must even-tually recognize what it is to BE Master of Vibration and this, Beloved Friends, constitutes RESPONSIBILITY.

You and you alone are responsible for your happiness!!! No one else, just you and this is where you must be honest with yourself and look within.

You have spent numerous lifetimes experienc-ing with vibration, are you ready to understand what it is to be Master of Vibration?

Ask yourself this question? How do I choose to Qualify Energy? With Life or Death?

Think on this. Are the actions I am taking support-ing LIFE or denying it? Are the thoughts I am thinking building up my life or the lives of others, or are my thoughts destroying life? Are the feelings I am feeling bringing more and more LIFE to me, to be all that I can be, or are those feelings taking more and more LIFE out of me? And here, I WILL emphasize, as you learn to become aware at any given moment what vibration you are expressing, you WILL KNOW if there is emo-tional attachment.

YOU MUST LET GO OF ALL EMOTIONAL ATTACH-MENTS!!!

Learn to become consciously aware of your thoughts, feelings and actions. Please remember this is practicing UNDIVIDED ATTENTION. Each time you practice Undivided Attention you will be 'Qualifying Life' with your Energy, AND the stronger LIFE grows within you.

This happens on a cellular level, my friends. This happens on a sub-atomic level and Divine Mind responds with more of the same, which is

Divine Vibration.

I AM BRINGING YOUR AWARENESS TO THE SPIRITUAL ASPECT OF THE LAW OF ATTRACTION.

And so the snowball effect grows. And before you know it you have a mountain of LIFE spilling out of your Being and still the snowball effect grows. And soon, those around you are affected by that dynamo you started, as you become consciously aware of QUALIFYING LIFE, in your HEART OF SACRED FIRE. (And you are flowing the Ascension Dimension)

My Brother, Beloved Ascended Master Sananda, called this 'Abundant Life', and So It Is!!

This is precisely how we escalate ourselves up this evolutionary ladder of consciousness. Energy has a vibration, which constitutes the Law of Attraction. All Energy is comprised of Vibration.

And how we choose to work with this Energy, dictates our experience!! And the Spiritual Aspect of the Law of Attraction holds the Frequency of the Ascension Dimension!!

There is a scientific and mathematical principle that manifests your Electronic Pattern and continues to magnetize more of the same. This principle, of which I refer to, is 'I AM'. You can use it to QUALIFY LIFE or (mis-)qualify death. It is your choice. No exceptions. It is the Law.

Please remember, the Qualification of Energy is a natural power in Heart of Sacred Fire, your Diamond Core God Cell, which is flowing the Ascension Dimension.

Let us take a common example. A person becomes weary with their life. Their circumstances become filled with negative expression and life becomes unbearable.

This then becomes their choice. Do they continue to choose what they have always had? *Or, do they change their focus? This is learning to consciously choose change.*

You have heard the old saying, "Keep doing what you are doing and you will keep getting the same". As long as you are able to come up with questions, which encourage excuses, you will stay in the drama!!

There comes a point in everyone's journey, the realization of taking responsibility!!

This is a grand step towards Spiritual Ascension.

Learn to take responsibility for your Energy AS YOU PRACTICE QUALIFYING LIFE. Please remember, Beloved Friends, either you are Master of Energy or Energy is Master of You. No exceptions. It is the Law. And as you Qualify Life, you are FLOWING in the ASCENSION DIMENSION, from Heart of Sacred Fire!!!

It is your energy, and you always have a choice how you choose to *Qualify your energy. You signed up for this job, it is in your contract, and sooner or later you have to meet yourself in the mirror and recognize it IS your energy, it IS your responsibility!!*

All Ascended Masters ARE Masters of Their Energy!!

The precise moment that you take full responsibility for your energy, that is the moment Angels sing a heavenly chord that resounds throughout the Universe of **Freedom.** It is the sweetest sound and those Angels that do this for you, are rejoicing in your hour of triumph.

Their Divine Sound weaves a fabric of Love and Light around your Etheric Body as you draw nearer and nearer to Divine Mind. This Heavenly Fabric is your Electronic Presence and it is comprised entirely of **Divine Vibration.** And it is Divine Vibration that creates your Light Body in the Ascension Dimension.

It would serve you greatly to connect with those Angels that sing for you in the Heavens, for they are holding a Divine Vibration of Love & Light for you. It is written. So Be It and So It Is.

DIVINE BLUEPRINT STEP FORWARD
DIVINE BLUEPRINT STEP FORWARD
DIVINE BLUEPRINT STEP FORWARD and BE, [I AM]

The Fifth Key

LIFE

Let us continue our discussion on **Divine Vibration.** It is within the layers of consciousness that vibration resides. *Vibration* is the essence of everything seen and unseen. It is that which manifests and yet it is that which resides in the unmanifested form. Consciousness is Source Energy and the essence of this Source is Vibration.

So, if you will, vibration makes the world go round. All that you see and all that you do not see carries vibration. Vibration is the 'Force' of Consciousness.

And from Source Energy, All That Is, Mother/Father God has evolved.

And from Mother/Father God, (Divine Mind) birthed **LIFE.**

This Divine Vibration known as **LIFE** is a most, glorious perfect blend of Love and Light, flowing into unlimited possibilities.

And it is this understanding that motivates **LIFE,** which is an extension of SOUL, to magnify and expand this Core Vibration, known as *Divine Vibration.*

It is this vibrational ladder that you climb, experiment upon and learn from which gives you a grander perspective of the Height, Depth and Volume of Mother/Father God.

Yes, My Dear Friends, as you increase your understanding of vibration, you recognize there is no limit to what you can achieve.

Vibration moves mountains, vibration creates universes, and vibration heals.

LIFE becomes your opportunity to expand from the position of unlimited possibilities. And, Beloved Friends, **LIFE** is Mother/Father God's gift to you.

LIFE is a most precious opportunity to express Divine Vibration. **LIFE** goes way beyond that skin upon your physical back.

LIFE is a sacred privilege pulsating with Divine Potential of 'I AM'.

Now, as one learns to experiment with **LIFE,** they recognize the opportunity to work with Divine Vibration puts one in the position of Co-Creating with Mother/Father God.

This path of enlightenment has become a most interesting evolutionary experiment for those who find themselves in embodiment now upon Beloved Terra. It has become an amazing plethora of "vibrational choices" for the novice as well as the adept.

And in those choices, you recognize to create from Unconditional Love brings a vibration of enlightenment, **Divine Vibration.**

Through trial and error you have come to recognize your Heart speaks strongly for that which lifts you up, and against that which tears you apart!!

It has been an evolutionary leap in Light Years from when this experiment began until NOW.

And I assure you, there are vast numbers in this Galaxy and numerous other Galaxies that are watching this Grand Experiment unfold on Beloved Terra.

As a matter of fact, I would like to add here, this Grand Experiment, **LIFE,** has been played out on Beloved Terra in a manner that will allow more SOUL Groups to evolve in the Love and Light of Mother/Father God, than any other planet.

I AM here to tell you, there is no other planet that will evolve more Ascended Masters than Beloved Terra and because of this She is and will be Honored Forever in the Great, Central Sun as the Queen of Hearts!!

For it is Beloved Terra that has held All within Her Bosom, Allowing Each SOUL to Safely Find Their Way Home. Thank You Beloved Terra, We Adore You!! So Be It and So It Is.

What you are coming to realize is your position in the scheme of things is critical for your Spiritual Ascension Process. It is vitally important that you recognize your approach, your awareness.

For those who choose the Ascension Dimension, your position is one of flexibility, stamina, courage, surrender, and most of all faith.

Faith in Mother/Father God is the Divine Vibration that will sustain you.

When you have no-thing left to pull from, when you recognize quietly in your Heart there is no more resistance left within you, you have arrived at sweet surrender. And your awareness takes in this Sacred Place known as NAK HEK NOL, ALL IS ONE.

This ancient, Galactic Light Language holds the Divine Vibration of your Light Body and Nature is bringing this forward now on Beloved Terra. It is this Galactic Light Language that Archangel Metatron originally created with Nature Consciousness to manifest 'I AM' on a cellular level within All of **LIFE.** Learn to listen to your Heart of Sacred Fire and you WILL hear this Galactic Light Language!!

And again I say, that which is not seen is more real and powerful than what is seen with the human eye! Learn to see through the ***Illusion.***

You recognize this place within your Heart Space is HEART OF SACRED FIRE. This is your Diamond Core God Cell, **I AM THAT I AM.**

It is that which carries your Divine Blueprint. This Divine Blueprint resides within every cell in your body, every electron, and vibrates your Spiritual Ascension, for Spiritual Ascension is FREEDOM.

And My Beloved Friends, this is **LIFE**.

I AM SANAT KUMARA, AND I STATE TO THE UNIVERSE, YOUR HEART OF SACRED FIRE HOLDS ALL THE KEYS TO YOUR SPIRITUAL ASCENSION. IT IS WITHIN THE SACRED FIRE THAT YOU WILL LEARN TO BE STILL, AND KNOW 'I AM'.

It is written. So Be It and So It Is.

There is no time within consciousness. We use this thing called 'time' to learn just how we want to vibrate, or experiment with a vibration. And a grand experiment it has become on Beloved Terra.

You are coming to recognize through countless reincarnations the **Illusion** of **time** is keeping you from that which you know to be your Heritage, your Divine Blueprint. Yes, the **Illusion** of **time** has served a purpose and is now growing old within your consciousness.

For eons of **'time'** you have expressed and experienced numerous vibrations in the Duality Consciousness. And those expressions and experiences have given you a grand perspective of limited frequency.

There are those of you who understand the need to become Unlimited in your experience, and take your rightful place as Co-Creators of Divine Vibration with Mother/Father God.

And so Now is THE pivotal moment. I said I would be here to remind you of this!

Your point of power is NOW. When does everything change? It changes when you take full responsibility for your Energy.

> ◢ *Either you are Master of your Energy or Energy is master of you.*
> ◢ *Either you are Master of your Energy or Energy is master of you.*
> ◢ *Either you are Master of your Energy or Energy is master of you.*

To manifest the Ascension Dimension, you must take full responsibility for your Energy, no matter what, and BE (I AM) within your Heart of Sacred Fire!!

*Remember, you have a choice at any given moment, which vibration you choose to experience. Whatever it is that you are going through. Whatever it is that you are experiencing. Whatever it is that you are needing or wanting or feeling, please remember. **NOW is your pivotal moment.** If you like where you are at NOW, then work on increasing that vibration. If you don't like where you are at right NOW, then work on changing that vibration to joy, love, light, peace.*

NOW can be your choice to create your FREEDOM!!

I would like to add, Beloved Terra, our Queen of Hearts, symbolizes the Spiritual Aspect of FREEDOM.

Dear brothers and sisters, your Heart of Sacred Fire, your Diamond Core God Cell is waiting for you. It is the most glorious gift that Mother/Father God has given and it is filled with **LIFE!!**

LIFE is that Divine Sacred Space where you can connect with your SOUL and experience Unconditional Love that Heals to the very core of your Beingness.

This journey we call *life* on Mother Earth, has given us the most incredible opportunities to become

Co-Creators with Mother/Father God.

Yes, this journey has provided us with countless experiences lifetime after lifetime to recognize FREE-DOM. This 3rd dimensional hologram we find ourselves in, echoes vibrations from Cosmic Multitudes and becomes our playground.

It is in this playground, life on Mother Earth, we get to choose!!!

Everyday, we get to choose which way we want to progress. Perhaps through the course of life, we decide we need more vibrational opportunities to continue the drama we choose to participate in. And so we move through that lifetime, on a see/saw, going up and down.

There is no judgment in the eyes of Mother/Father God, just experience. All moves us in a direction. That direction, Beloved Friends, is your opportunity to choose a vibration.

You may choose a vibration of discord and continue to participate in that drama and all the experiences that would go with that avenue.

And when you have done that enough, you begin to recognize the ***ILLUSION.***

Yes, when you have participated in that drama enough, you begin to think,

"Aahh, perhaps there is a better way to go about my business?"

And so you begin the task of taking responsibility, to raise your vibration in the direction of FREE-DOM, AS YOU BECOME MASTER OF ENERGY and FLOW IN THE ASCENSION DIMENSION.

What DOES Freedom mean to you?

For Me, it holds a Sacred Space of Allowing Me to pursue LIFE in the manner that brings me the greatest JOY and PEACE OF MIND.

As you learn to sit quietly with Heart of Sacred Fire, meditate and ask questions. What does my Heart say to me? Am I allowing Joy in my Life? Am I allowing Unconditional Love, which means Love without judgment, pure, not requiring anything in return, to flow from my Heart towards all? Am I allowing my Heart to speak those feelings that I need to listen to?

Beloved Friends, the only salvation that is important to your Enlightenment is FREEDOM in your Vibrational Alignment with Divine Mind! This FREEDOM is Divine Alignment with 'I AM', and allows us to create Joy, Love and Light which is your Divine Birthright that SOUL nudges you, lifetime after lifetime to fulfill your destiny and manifest your Divine Blueprint.

Mankind has experienced through countless lifetimes, a vibration. Everything has a vibration. It is the core of Universal Consciousness.

And Mother/Father God created LIFE. And with that LIFE, Mother/Father God allows All to experience vibration.

LIFE is the perfect balance of Light and Love. It is the synergy that motivates everything to expand. The Yin and the Yang, the moving and flowing. It is the core essence of your experience. This thing called consciousness, this thing called freedom; this thing called love, there is a vibration.

And LIFE (core essence) allows you to experience ALL and express the Divine Vibration of FREEDOM, which is 'I AM'.

For in this **Divine Vibration of FREEDOM** you will learn to recognize that Mother/Father God gives you **LIFE,** and **LIFE MORE ABUNDANTLY.** Through this journey of vibration, you will learn to **FEEL YOUR WAY TO FREEDOM.**

Those feelings will guide you into your **Heart of Sacred Fire, your Diamond Core God Cell, I AM THAT I AM!!**

Remember, the Qualification of Energy is a natu-ral power within your Heart of Sacred Fire, which automatically flows you in the Ascension Dimension.

And as you learn to feel this Divine Vibration of Mother/Father God in your Heart of Sacred Fire, WHICH IS LIFE, it will ILLUMINATE YOUR EXISTENCE. IT WILL ILLUMINATE YOUR JOURNEY, IT WILL MAG-NETICALLY QUALIFY YOU WITH ALL THAT IS HOLY, and this IS ABUNDANT LIFE. It is that which has driven mankind from the Beginning, the search for the Holy Grail, which is ABUNDANT LIFE and it has always been your Diamond Core God Cell!!!!!!!

To express Abundant Life is the greatest privilege that SOUL has been given, and it starts and stops within your Heart of Sacred Fire.

It is written. So Be It and So It Is.

And you will move forward in the Love and Light of Mother/Father God.

And I assure you, it is a journey that has no begin-ning and no ending. It is a journey that goes on forever.

And the more that you learn to *Qualify your vibra-tion with LIFE,* the more you will understand, that you will not let anyone or anything rob you ever again, of your Destiny, your Divine Birthright as Co-Creators of *Divine Vibration* with Mother/Father God in your Heart of Sacred Fire, flowing the Ascension Dimension.

DIVINE BLUEPRINT STEP FORWARD
DIVINE BLUEPRINT STEP FORWARD
DIVINE BLUEPRINT STEP FORWARD and BE, [I AM]

The Sixth Key

THE SPIRITUAL ASPECT OF THE LAW OF ATTRACTION

And now I am going to share with you a most glorious truth that only few have been able to receive. *This truth holds the most significant energy for your Spiritual Ascension.*

***THE SPIRITUAL ASPECT OF THE LAW OF ATTRACTION IS DIVINE VIBRATION. AND DIVINE VIBRATION IS QUALIFIED LIFE.** Every Spiritual Student must learn to manifest with Divine Vibration (Qualified Life) in order to connect with their Light Body 24/7, MOVING FROM THEIR HEART OF SACRED FIRE.*

Please read those words over and over, meditate on them and call on my Ascended Energy to assist you in opening up to this monumental truth. For Divine Vibration flowing from Heart of Sacred Fire WILL bring Heaven within you and manifest your Adam Kadmon Light Body. I AM SANAT KUMARA AND I WILL BE THERE TO ASSIST YOU.
So Be It and So It Is.

As you read through this book, I will discuss various ways to manifest, increase and expand Divine Vibration. **Focus on these words 'Divine Vibration'.**

You have an understanding of the Law of Attraction; it has been brought to the forefront by Ascended Masters of the Light, known as 'Abraham'.

They have, most wondrously shared information

47

on the Law of Attraction, which has benefited multitudes in glorious ways.

I have chosen to share with you the *'Spiritual Aspect of the Law of Attraction = Divine Vibration'*.

It comes from your Heart of Sacred Fire and carries the frequency of Unconditional Love and Light. I will teach you in experimenting with Source Energy, how to work with it from a **Divine Vantage Point.**

- **To QUALIFY ENERGY = LIFE**

- **To MIS-QUALIFY ENERGY = DEATH**

No exceptions. It is written. So Be It. And So It Is.

I am going to share with you Ascended Master truths.

- All Energy IS, Source Energy.
- I AM THAT I AM is Mother/Father God Energy.
- **I AM holds an Electronic Current of Magnetic Energy that is unequaled throughout the Universe, of Divine Vibration.**
- The Qualification of Energy is a natural power within your Heart of Sacred Fire (Diamond Core God Cell)
- From SOUL, you agreed to learn how to expand 'I AM' Energy with Divine Vibration from your Heart of Sacred Fire

  - ❖ *As you expand that Energy, you recognize Qualified or (Mis)-Qualified.*
  - ❖ **QUALIFIED ENERGY IS LIFE**
  - ❖ **MIS-QUALIFIED ENERGY IS DEATH**

You said you would experiment with expanded vibration and learn to QUALIFY LIFE IN ALL THINGS. And as you allow the QUALIFYING OF LIFE, YOU MANIFEST THE WILL OF MOTHER/FATHER GOD. And as the Will of Mother/Father God is manifested on Beloved Terra, Heaven on Earth shines through YOU!!

'QUALIFIED LIFE' FROM YOUR HEART OF SACRED FIRE, IS THE SACRED SPIRITUAL FORMULA MOTHER/FATHER GOD CREATED.'

Think on these words that I am sharing with you. **QUALIFIED LIFE:**

- A Spiritual Formula that holds Eternal Life.
- A Spiritual Formula that manifests Divine Vibration.
- A Spiritual Formula that manifests your Heart's Desires.
- A Spiritual Formula that holds Divine Potential.
- A Spiritual Formula that scientifically and mathematically manifests the Highest Vibration from Divine Mind, the Ascension Dimension.

Qualified Life is THE Sacred Union of Love and Light personified as Divine Vibration within Heart of Sacred Fire. Divine Vibration IS Qualified Life. Qualified Life is Divine Vibration.

How does one learn to Qualify Life? Remember, as you Qualify Energy you create Life. As you (Mis)-Qualify Energy you create death.

I would like to point out here; I am speaking of LIFE on All Levels. This physical expression that you refer to as life is just a mere pinpoint of your Cosmic Beingness. (I will expand on this in greater detail in Chapter 17, Ascended Masters.)

Each day that you live, from the second you open your eyes, to the moment you close them and sleep at the end of your day, you have opportunity after opportunity to Qualify Life and become Master of Energy through Divine Vibration.

- QUALIFY LIFE THROUGH APPRECIATION
- QUALIFY LIFE THROUGH RESPECT
- QUALIFY LIFE THROUGH JOY
- QUALIFY LIFE THROUGH HONOR
- QUALIFY LIFE THROUGH INTEGRITY
- QUALIFY LIFE THROUGH GRATITUDE
- QUALIFY LIFE THROUGH PEACE
- QUALIFY LIFE THROUGH SINCERITY
- QUALIFY LIFE THROUGH THANKFULNESS
- QUALIFY LIFE THROUGH KINDNESS
- QUALIFY LIFE THROUGH LOVE
- **QUALIFY LIFE THROUGH YOUR HEART of SACRED FIRE, DIAMOND CORE GOD CELL, I AM THAT I AM**

You will learn to move from your Ascension Dimension Cord, between your 3rd Eye and your Heart of Sacred Fire. *All of your Energy needs to move out from that Sacred Space, as you are practicing Qualifying Life.* You will learn to understand Energy moving out from Lower Chakras, or Lower Ego, is not conducive for the Ascension Dimension. Lower Ego holds the *Illusion* Vibration, and your *Heart of Sacred Fire* Space holds the *Ascension Dimension.* (Call upon Me and I will assist you).

I am going to challenge you, from this moment forward, do not let a moment go by ever again, that you are not aware of QUALIFYING LIFE. Call upon my Ascended Energy and I will assist you to QUALIFY LIFE. This comes from your Heart of Sacred Fire. (Remember, the Qualification of Energy is a natural power within your Heart of Sacred Fire), AND FLOW IN THE ASCENSION DIMENSION.

DIVINE BLUEPRINT STEP FORWARD
DIVINE BLUEPRINT STEP FORWARD
DIVINE BLUEPRINT STEP FORWARD and BE, [I AM]

The Seventh Key

DIVINE ALIGNMENT

Qualifying Life requires taking responsibility, and Mastering your Energy. As you take responsibility for your Energy, you learn to TEST the vibration. Testing the vibration brings DIVINE ALIGNMENT. And your *Desires* allow you to create with Source Energy from Divine Intention, which brings you into DIVINE ALIGNMENT.

LEARN TO 'SET DIVINE INTENTION' WITHIN ENERGY AND ALL WILL BE IN DIVINE ALIGNMENT, as you move from your HEART OF SACRED FIRE.

Let us discuss 'testing the vibration' from a Divine Vantage Point.

Always ask yourself this question? What am I feeling as my day progresses? Does this feeling or do these feelings bring me Joy? If your answer is yes, you are Qualifying Life.

If your answer is no, you are (Mis)-Qualifying Death.

Asking these questions brings one into Divine Alignment, which starts and stops in your Heart of Sacred Fire. It is absolutely essential to remain in Divine Alignment as you learn to move from 3D to 5D.

(Divine Alignment starts in your Heart of Sacred Fire, and flows the Ascension Dimension Cord between Heart and 3rd Eye.)

Are you finished with 3D?

3D is the path of reincarnation. Are you done with the birth and death cycle?

3D is the **Illusion.**

3D has provided you with a myriad of opportunities to experience lust, poverty, fear and conditional love.

3D has been the 'test' to recognize Light versus Darkness.

3D has given you the **Illusion of Duality, opposite poles of negative and positive.**

3D has allowed you to experience separation from that which created you.

3D keeps you stuck in the Lower Chakras.

Are you finished with 3D?

It is important to add here; moving away from 3D can seem as if you are in a fog.

Almost, surreal, at moments. You may wake up in the morning and feel like you are not in your physical body, and yet you know it is your body. It may seem like hours before you feel like all parts of you have come back into alignment in your physical body and you feel together. This IS the old paradigm dying off and the new, enlightened frequencies solidifying within your Beingness. It can seem very disorienting, strange and humbling all at the same time. You are literally being re-wired and your physical body is catching up.

Call on your Angels and My Ascended Energy and We will surround you and protect you as this progress takes place.

What Is 5D? And what happened to 4D? And how many 'D's' are there?

My Dear Friends, I remember very well a time when I asked Myself these questions.

In 4D you have recognized the old paradigms are keeping you in the ***Illusion of separation from that which created you.*** It is in this recognition that one takes responsibility, and learns to Master their Energy. 4D is the doorway to your Electronic Light Presence.

In 4D you are moving away from lack, fear and separation.

In 4D you are understanding how to utilize these transformational keys for your Spiritual Ascension.

In 4D you recognize that which cheats you of LIFE.

In 4D you understand there is Darkness, and so YOU CHOOSE Lightness

In 4D you are taking responsibility for your Energy and refusing to participate in the ***Illusion.***

In 5D you have earned the privilege of your Light Body.

In 5D you reside within your Heart of Sacred Fire, graced with At-one-ment by that which created you, Mother/Father God.

In 5D you Co-Create from your Heart in Unconditional Love, non-judgmentally.

In 5D you move as One with Divine Mind and you experience pure Joy in God's Will.

In 5D your Divine Vibration is 'I AM' with Mother/Father God, and you REST (BE) in your Heart of Sacred Fire.

I will discuss the Higher Dimensions in Chapter 17 'Ascended Masters'.

LEARN TO 'SET DIVINE INTENTION' WITHIN ENERGY from your HEART OF SACRED FIRE, AND ALL WILL BE IN DIVINE ALIGNMENT.

Take responsibility for your Energy. Each moment of your day, ask yourself, how do I feel? Am I Qualifying Life, or (Mis)-Qualifying Death? Learn to become aware of your vibration and you will KNOW if there is emotional attachment. These questions bring you into Divine Alignment as you become Master of Energy.

As we Honor the Divinity within Energy, all Illusions become no-thing. Showing the Universe your APPRECIATION, your GRATITUDE your THANKFULNESS, will bring Showers of Blessings unequaled in any other Realm. And the Divine Vibration of APPRECIATION will bring you into Divine Alignment faster than anything else. THANKSGIVING IS the pouring forth of your Qualified Energy, which automatically connects you with your Causal Body.

(This is a big plus, with all the Bells and Whistles that go with Causal Body.)

LEARN TO 'SET DIVINE INTENTION' WITHIN ENERGY from your HEART OF SACRED FIRE, AND ALL WILL BE IN DIVINE ALIGNMENT.

Your journey of remembering All That You Are brings you into Divine Alignment with Mother/Father God.

Respect for Energy will bring you to a Sacred Space of honoring the Divine. It is awareness, and it moves you towards LIFE. I cannot emphasize enough the importance within the English word **'Respect'**. To show *respect* for the momentum that Energy carries, allows you to see from a Divine Vantage Point.

And as you practice Divine Vibration, Qualifying Life from your Heart of Sacred Fire, with the Spiritual Aspect of the Law of Attraction you honor the Divinity within Energy. This brings you into Divine Alignment, which is absolutely essential for manifesting your Light Body.

If there are ***Illusions*** that stand between you and your Hearts Desires, you are NOT IN DIVINE ALIGNMENT!! You must learn to move away from Lower Ego and into Divine Alignment as you flow the Ascension Dimension. And once again, I repeat:

LEARN TO 'SET DIVINE INTENTION' WITHIN ENERGY from your HEART OF SACRED FIRE, AND ALL WILL BE IN DIVINE ALIGNMENT.

> ✍ **As you CONSCIOUSLY practice setting Divine Intention within your desires, within your Energy, within all that you do, throughout your day, ALL WILL BE BROUGHT INTO DIVINE ALIGNMENT. *AS YOU CREATE GOD'S WILL FROM YOUR HEART OF SACRED FIRE, ALL ENERGIES ARE ASSISTED TO MOVE INTO DIVINE ALIGNMENT, AND IF THEY DO NOT ALIGN, THEY WILL LEAVE!!* (And you will flow the Ascension Dimension)**
>
> It is here, My Dear Friends, you can make a most Glorious Pivotal Turn towards your Freedom. Please Read this over and over!!!

Your desires are part and parcel of your journey in 3D. It is through your desires that you learn what it is to manifest the Will of God in your Life and Qualify Life. (This is BE-ING Unconditional Love from your Heart of Sacred Fire.)

Do not ever negate your desires!! Your Desires are synchronistic ally planned to allow you to manifest Divine Vibration, which ultimately leads you into Divine Alignment, moving within and from your Heart of Sacred Fire.

And so My Dear Friends, I encourage you to pursue the Desires of Your Heart.

It is those Desires that also become your Teachers, (which I discuss in length in Chapter 16, Higher Self).

This is how you learn to Master Your Energy and create your Light Body.

Ask for My assistance with this, and I will bring it into the Light for you to understand from a Divine Vantage Point.

DIVINE BLUEPRINT STEP FORWARD
DIVINE BLUEPRINT STEP FORWARD
DIVINE BLUEPRINT STEP FORWARD and BE, [I AM]

The Eighth Key

FREE WILL – CHOICE

Freedom of choice. This comes with a price.

And for those of you who have reincarnated numerous times, your SOUL is guiding you now to take full responsibility for your choices.

There is a song that has within it, "I did it my way". I am here to tell you now; there are many paths of consciousness.

And there are some paths that are easier than others, and there are some paths that bring more joy or less joy.

And there are some paths that lead to a dead end, because that individual refused to take responsibility for their actions!!

It is always your choice, your free will. What you have to ask yourself is this. "Do I like where I am at in my life?" "Am I at peace with myself?" "Have I honored my feelings in all matters?" which is another way of saying, "To Thine Own Self, Be True."

These are questions you need to ask yourself, with *sincerity from your Heart.*

You have heard the saying "Action speaks louder than words".

The Universe knows this phrase more clearly than even you can imagine!!!

Action manifests everything; words hold the vibration of the feeling that backs them up.

Action is the vibration of feeling, and as one expresses the energy of action, the vibration increases with that action energy, which is the Law of Attraction.

And in this 3D Illusion, you said you would participate with the Law of Attraction through Free Will – Choice.

And for some, this 3D Illusion has left you feeling spiritually bankrupt!

Time is drawing to an end for the Illusion of 3D. Time as you have known it will change.

For Beloved Terra is slated for 5D.

You said you would come back in this time and in this space and **understand what it is to take full responsibility for your actions!! And so you shall!!**

This is where you move away from spiritual bankruptcy and start filling your actions with Qualified Life.

This is where you DECIDE whether or not this is your final Destiny with Birth and Death!!

And you said you would do this through Free Will, learning to make choices through your own Free Will. **This involves, your words, your thoughts, your feelings, your Qualified LIFE.**

You are thinking right now, I can't do this Sanat; it is too much for me. I can't do this.

And I am here to tell you now, YES, you can!! You can do this, as many before you have already done this. It starts and stops with you. Call on my Ascended Energy and I will guide you, in Love and bring Peace to your Heart.

(Please remember, My Energy is the color Peach, which vibrates the Ascension Dimension.)

EACH CIRCUMSTANCE IN YOUR LIFE, GIVES YOU A GOLDEN OPPORTUNITY TO TAKE FULL RESPONSIBILITY, AS YOU LEARN TO QUALIFY LIFE OF YOUR OWN FREE WILL.

And again, I say, To Thine Own Self Be True. Do not become complacent with your life as it is. Always, Always,

Always, go within your Heart and ask "Am I Qualifying Life, or am I (Mis)-Qualifying Death with my choices?"

"Where have my free will and choices gotten me?"

It is time to ask yourself, when do I get these lessons? How long do I keep repeating behavior that (Mis)-Qualifies = Death?

My Dear Friends, I would like to bring LIGHT to your lessons. You have asked yourself countless times, through numerous incarnations, what is this all about? Your lessons are your teachers. And those teachers are here because you created them. Think on this for a moment. Anything and everything in your life that is an issue, a project, a problem, a bother; those are your Teachers.

Mother Earth is known as the school for the Gods, and you have created *'Teachers'*. And those Teachers will not leave until you get what it is you said you would get. (I will cover more of this subject in the Chapter 16, Higher Self.)

Are you getting the picture? Those things in your life that you DON'T LIKE, LOOK THEM HARD IN THE EYES AND YOU WILL SEE YOURSELF.

I Love you My Friends, and I want to soften that statement with the Love of Mother/Father God. It is very hard to admit that we create our reality, and then to throw on top of that heap, all of those painful issues we have created, are our Teachers. Very hard, indeed!

And now, take the next step with Free Will and Choice and Qualify Life from your Heart of Sacred Fire!! (Remember to flow with your Ascension Dimension Cord, which I explain in the Heart of Sacred Fire Meditation.)

The very fact that Mother/Father God has given us all Free Will to choose is a most glorious and gracious gesture that has been misunderstood and abused through centuries of life streams.

It is time to wake up!!

- This is your opportunity NOW to choose that which QUALIFIES LIFE.
- This is your opportunity NOW to choose that which is HONORABLE.
- This is your opportunity NOW to choose that which is RESPECTFUL.
- This is your opportunity NOW to choose that which is RIGHT-USE-NESS.
- This is your opportunity NOW to choose that which is JOY.
- This is your opportunity NOW to choose that which brings LOVE AND LIGHT.
- This is your opportunity NOW to manifest your DIVINE BLUEPRINT.
- This is your opportunity NOW to consciously connect with your Light Body.
- This is your opportunity NOW to REST (BE) in your Heart of Sacred Fire.

You sat with your Spiritual Counsel; SOUL, Higher Self, and reviewed your Divine Blueprint. There are those of you who came to fulfill old debts and there are those of you who came to assist your SOUL Group and the Collective Consciousness. This is your Sacred Contract. You said you would do this!

And I said I would help you remember! And with that remembering, I said I would be here to assist you to QUALIFY LIFE FROM YOUR HEART OF SACRED FIRE, which is flowing the ASCENSION DIMENSION!!!

You have heard the phrase, "When the going gets tough, the tough get going!" It is now time to get going!!

Each individual must wake up, and let go of the complacency from lifetime after lifetime of old, ineffective programs ingrained on a subconscious level.

Those old programs are within the cells, however, I Beloved Sanat Kumara, would like to share with you a most glorious spiritual truth.

Your Electronic Light Body is the Winner of this Race. Your Electronic Light Body holds the Electronic Pattern within your Electrons of 'I AM' Divine Vibration. This is truth from Divine Mind. And your Cells know, if any programming is contrary to Divine Mind, your Cells KNOW, they HAVE to get it right. Your Cells carry tiny Electrons of Light which hold the perfection of Divine Mind, housed within your Diamond Core God Cell, beautifully packaged in your Heart of Sacred Fire.

Sooner or later, no matter how many choices you make; sooner or later, your Cells KNOW they have to get it right. And your cells know, Free Will and Choice is in their Sacred Contract to connect with Electronic Light Presence, allowing Diamond Core God Cell, I AM THAT I AM to Reign Supreme on Earth as it is in Heaven.

It is Written. So Be It & So It Is.

I can hear you saying, "How do I change?" "I don't know how to change my life?"

It is now time to look at your choices. Start with today. And each step that you take let it be a choice of Qualifying Life, through your Free Will and Choice.

Sincerely look at your choices and make

decisions based upon Qualifying Life!!

No longer look to anyone or anything to bring you happiness. YOUR HAPPINESS STARTS AND STOPS WITH YOU. NO ONE IS RESPONSIBLE FOR YOUR HAPPINESS, EXCEPT YOU!!!

You can change. It is possible to change. It starts with one thing. Pick one thing that you feel you would like to change. Look at that one thing from your Heart. This is a sincere space, a humble space. This is not a space of condemnation, nor regrets. This is a space of loving, sincerity. You are not judged for your life. You are not condemned for your life. Do not allow yourself to criticize (your life), nor feel guilt over things already done.

It is a precious waste of your energy.

Mother/Father God does not judge, nor condemn, so why do you?

Again, I say to you, QUALIFY LIFE AND MASTER YOUR ENERGY in your Heart of Sacred Fire, and flow your Ascension Dimension Cord!!!

- Mother/Father God is waiting for you to wake up.
- The Spiritual Hierarchy is waiting for you to wake up.
- SOUL is waiting for you to wake up.

Stop slumbering, stop the complacency, stop the regrets, stop the guilt, stop the condemnation, and stop the judgment. You **DO NOT** have time for this anymore!! You have spent enough hours, throughout this life and many other lifetimes filled with regrets. No more!

It stops when you say, ENOUGH!

TAKE THE STEPS NOW TO QUALIFY LIFE FROM YOUR HEART OF SACRED FIRE, AND LIVE IN JOY, LOVE AND LIGHT AS YOU PRACTICE YOUR FREE WILL OF CHOICES!!

As the individual learns to take responsibility for their choices, through Free Will, a great Wisdom sets in for them on all levels. This is the ***Divine Wisdom of SOUL*** and it carries you Home. As you practice this, My Dear Friends, you will recognize and appreciate this ***Divine Wisdom of SOUL.***

It feels right in your Heart. It rests in your Heart. It creates En-Light-In-Ment in your Heart. The ***Divine Wisdom of SOUL*** is your Heritage. And you find it through making choices, based on Free Will, of Qualifying Life from your Heart of Sacred Fire. And remember the Qualification of Energy is a natural power within your Heart. ALL, brings us back to our Heart of Sacred Fire, Diamond Core God Cell, I AM THAT I AM.

DIVINE BLUEPRINT STEP FORWARD
DIVINE BLUEPRINT STEP FORWARD
DIVINE BLUEPRINT STEP FORWARD and BE, [I AM]

The Ninth Key

UNCONDITIONAL LOVE

Because of the great spiritual value that Unconditional Love brings to the Spiritual Ascension student, I AM devoting an entire chapter to bring this to your attention. This chapter is a ***must-read*** for the serious spiritual student, for Unconditional Love is the Allowing/BE-ing which ALL must come home to.

This Energy known as Unconditional Love constitutes the fabric of the walls that house your Heart of Sacred Fire.

Unconditional Love is THE REDEEMING VIBRATION OF MOTHER/FATHER GOD.
Unconditional Love is THE REDEEMING VIBRATION OF MOTHER/FATHER GOD.
Unconditional Love is THE REDEEMING VIBRATION OF MOTHER/FATHER GOD.
It is Written. So Be it and So It Is.
Please read that statement over and over and over.

This Energy is the Feminine Essence of Mother/Father God and it literally moves mountains and makes the blind to see. It is this Unconditional Love that mankind has bargained with, fought, pleaded and refused since Time was created, and it is that which will bring mankind to its knees in the End.

There is no greater Energy within the Universe, than ***Unconditional Love*** and it gives Me the greatest joy to share with you that ***Mother/Father God IS Unconditional Love.***

Imagine that, my Dear Friends, Unconditional Love will fill your Spiritual Bank and leave you wanting for NO-THING.

It will BE, That Which Stands when all else fails, without judgment, **PURE,** for the Heavens will sing a Divine Chord which will be heard throughout all Infinity, that Mother/Father God, '**I AM**', is *Unconditional Love.*

The musical note of *Unconditional Love* is a Divine Sound that creates Joy, Harmony, Peace, Well-Being and Appreciation.

There are Glorious Angels that sing this song of *Unconditional Love* and if you could for a moment, open your Inner Ear, what you would hear would literally bring you to your knees and allow all to fall at your feet. For this Redeeming, Divine Vibration known as Unconditional Love holds a vibration that is Pure, All-Knowing, wanting nothing, complete.

And those that bow will **KNOW LIFE,** and those that do not acknowledge *Unconditional Love,* they **DO NOT HAVE LIFE.**

And I would like to add here, it does not matter where you are in your evolution, when that Divine Heavenly Chord is sung, everyone shall hear it!!

Not all will acknowledge it, yet, everyone WILL HEAR IT!!!

It is written. So Be It and So It Is.

I share these words with you to create a picture for you to hold in your Heart.

And now to the practicality of applying this in your everyday lives. It seems as We, the Ascended Masters have observed mankind move through their lessons, there is a belief that God wants one to be the martyr for their loved ones.

My Dear Friends, I assure you, that is not Unconditional Love. You will learn first in your journey of Spiritual Ascension to come from a place of *JOY,* no matter what, is essential for your empowerment.

- Victim/Martyr is 3D
- Victim/Martyr is the Illusion
- Victim/Martyr is (Mis)-Qualified energy = death.

You must learn to draw healthy, boundaries for yourself with your Loved Ones.

From this, you will recognize Unconditional Love (God's Will) flows from your Heart, without judgment. Does this mean you become a rug for others to walk on? Absolutely not!

Once again, you understand there is a vibration and which vibration do you choose?

And here, I will add, sometimes emotional pain is experienced to identify a vibration, for the purpose of SOUL Growth. (No one said this was going to be easy!! And yet, if it were always easy, you would not grow!!!) Let us talk about your Loved One's. You know who I am referring to. Those in your life that hold a space in your Heart that bring you joy.

And now I am hearing, what about those Loved One's that don't bring me Joy? Here we get to the nuts and bolts of Unconditional Love.

You can't change someone's energy, (if you try taking on their energy it becomes your energy and you know the rest of that story)!

OH, those dynamics of Love. How those dynamics can grab your attention faster than anything else. It is those lessons of Love that will teach you, very quickly, what it is that you don't want!!

You know that which I speak of, for I can hear you now saying, 'Yes, that is so true!'

You are not allowed to change someone else's energy or free will. If you do, you take on their karmic debts, DON'T GO THERE!!!!

It is enough to Master your Energy, don't personalize their energy, then it becomes yours!

IF, you can come to a space in your Heart of Sacred Fire of practicing Unconditional Love for someone, which is holding a space of non-judgment, you are Qualifying Life.

And Buddha so wonderfully put it "no-attachments"!! This is where you recognize, letting go of all emotional attachments becomes your Freedom!!

It is very important that you understand what I am sharing with you.

As you hold a space of non-judgment for that loved one or someone significant in your life (this also includes co-workers, friends etc.), YOU ARE TOTALLY LETTING GO AND LETTING GOD DO THAT WHICH IS FOR THEIR HIGHEST GOOD!! NO EXCEPTIONS!!

YOUR OPINION OF WHAT SHOULD OR SHOULD NOT HAPPEN DOES NOT MATTER!! **ALL THAT MATTERS IS THE WILL OF GOD!!!!!!**

CAN YOU DO THAT?

HAVE YOU COME TO A PLACE WHERE YOU ARE ABSOLUTELY EXHAUSTED?

ARE YOU READY TO LET GO OF THE GUILT?

ARE YOU READY TO LET GO OF THE JUDGEMENT?

ARE YOU READY TO LET GO OF YOUR LOWER-EGO?

CAN YOU TOTALLY LET GO AND LET GOD?

These are hard questions and I send you My Love & Light as you read them and are totally honest with yourself. I bless you with glorious Love and Light and honor your ability to move forward in the Love and Light of Mother/Father God.
And from that space within your Heart of Sacred Fire, YOU ABSOLUTELY ASSIST THAT PERSON TO MOVE FORWARD IN THE LOVE AND LIGHT OF MOTHER/ FATHER GOD.

Yes, as you are able to let go of all emotional attachments, you allow those individuals to move forward in the Love and Light of Mother/Father God.

It is here that I will discuss *Guilt.* I could spend an entire chapter talking about guilt.

If one were to look within the Akashic Records, your Eternal Diary, you would observe millions and millions of life streams who have wasted much energy in that expression known as *Guilt.*

I would like to remind you; even the word 'waste' has a vibration. And, as I have pointed out, all is a vibration. You came to experience vibration, and there are those of you who came to experience vibration from the Divine Vantage Point of Qualifying Life.

So, hear me now, as I speak this to your Cosmic Beingness, please hear the 'Bigger Picture.'

- GUILT IS NOT OF MOTHER/FATHER GOD. NEVER WAS, NEVER WILL BE.
- GUILT WAS ALLOWED FOR THE PURPOSE OF EXPERIENCE.
- GUILT WILL ROB YOU OF JOY; GUILT WILL ROB YOU OF LIGHT.

- GUILT WILL ROB YOU OF GODS REDEEMING LOVE.
- GUILT WILL FILL YOU WITH DOUBT, UNWORTHINESS AND HOPELESSNESS.

I have taken the time to create a picture for you to understand how this vibration known as *'Guilt'* has stood between you and Your Destiny. It has been a test that you all agreed to participate in.

You have My Word on that! You ALL Agreed To Participate!!

And because of this amazing journey on Beloved Terra, MUCH, for lack of a better term, MUCH will be established as a precedent for future generations within the Universe to learn from Our Beloved Mother Earth, We Love and Honor Her!!!!

UNCONDITONAL LOVE IS THE REDEEMING Vibration that can only come from your Heart of Sacred Fire. It is a Sacred Space of Non-Judgment, pure and requiring NO-THING.

And, it comes in color! Violet, Gold and Pink. Violet is the Holy Spirit. Gold is Unconditional Love. Pink is Love, Divine Feminine Energy.

- Unconditional Love is a requirement for Spiritual Ascension, because it holds the Redeeming Vibration of Mother/Father God's, Diamond Core God Cell.
- Unconditional Love is a requirement to be Co-Creators with Mother/Father God.
- Unconditional Love is a requirement to become Master of Energy.
- Unconditional Love is a requirement to Qualify Life.

- Unconditional Love is a requirement to let go of judgment.
- Unconditional Love is a requirement to move beyond the Illusion.
- ***Unconditional Love is the Divine Vibration within your Heart of Sacred Fire, flowing your Ascension Dimension Cord, which manifests your Merkabah.***

My Dear Friends, one must cultivate and practice this Holy Space of Redeeming Vibration that holds Unconditional Love. For as you do this, you will recognize, it is not of 3D.

It is of Divine Mind and is given in grace to those who are open to receive.

You will KNOW that which I speak of, for you will find, you will go down on your knees to serve in JOY that which created you, Mother/Father God. For there is no greater service than to give your Heart to Mother/Father God in JOY, and it is that Holy Space known as Unconditional Love.

AND it absolutely comes from your Heart of Sacred Fire, as you practice Qualifying Life, you are BEING Unconditional Love. So Be It and So It Is.

DIVINE BLUEPRINT STEP FORWARD
DIVINE BLUEPRINT STEP FORWARD
DIVINE BLUEPRINT STEP FORWARD and BE, [I AM]

The Tenth Key

FAITH = THE WILL OF GOD

Faith is the essence of things hoped for, the evidence of things not yet seen. Hope is the 'looking glass' into JOY.

And as you can see in the title of this chapter, Faith Equals The Will of God.

My Dear Friends, I am here to share with you, Faith is the joy-filled momentum which brings you back home to that which created you. Faith is an essence so beautiful to behold, that were mankind to look upon Her, he/she would know that all is well and there is naught to worry about.

Yes, My Dear Friends, ***Faith*** is of the Royal Angelic Realm, Twin Flame of Archangel Michael and My Beloved Sister.

She holds the Eternal Vigil of Hope with Beloved Archangel Michael and fans that flame within the Heart of Mankind whenever it reaches a low point. Her Sacred Vow whispers in your Inner Ear of Hope that dawns eternal.

It is She who ministers to your broken Hearts in your hour of deepest need. And it is ***Faith*** that lovingly builds a momentum of Divine Vibration to remind you of your Divine Blueprint.

Faith and Archangel Michael have picked you up and steadied you so that you could continue to move forward, even when you did not know how you could possibly take another step.

Faith and Archangel Michael carry the Sacred Vow of God's Will on Mother Earth since Time began and they will continue to do so until Heaven is manifested on Beloved Terra.

This will be known as the Golden Age of Enlightenment. This Glorious Era will be the Divine Union of Humans working with Angels & Nature manifesting God's Will.

Were I to give you words of encouragement, I would say to you, find that 'Looking Glass'. It is called Hope and Faith will help you find it.

It is the 'Looking Glass' of Trust that will quiet your Heart and give you a peace which passes all understanding. My Dear Friends, your trust, your faith is the only way to remember that which you have forgotten.

There may be times when you cannot even see your hand in front of your face. And yet, your Heart tells you that your hand is there, even though your eyes cannot see it. That is Faith and it keeps you sustained. Faith is the Hope of a brighter day! Faith that God is watching! Faith, knowing Angels of Love and Light are hovering near, even though you cannot see them. Your Heart tells you this is truth, and that is Faith.

Faith PULLS you forward!!
There comes a point in the journey of every spiritual student of total vulnerability.
This IS childlike FAITH. Total surrender and trust to that which created you. That, My Dear Friends, is TRUST and it carries the Divine Vibration, known as FAITH. The very second that you go down on your knees within your Heart of Sacred Fire and say, I serve you Mother/Father God, in JOY, I serve you, you KNOW, in that moment, nothing else matters! That is total surrender!!

It is that decision, made in the quietness of your Heart that Heaven is created within you. Yes, My Dear Friends, Heaven is created within you, at the precise second, when you make THE decision that nothing else matters, only that you serve Mother/Father God in Joy. That is Faith's triumphant call, a Heavenly Chord is sung and the Light of All That Is shines on you with JOY, SWEET JOY and you will KNOW when this is done within your Heart, for you FEEL your Angels smiling with you!!

You understand this path back to that which created you is sometimes lonely. And still, it is Faith that reassures you, All Is Well. (And you feel vulnerable as a child) This is Good, my Dear Friends, This is Good!! This is known as a humble spirit, and I assure you, it comes deep within the Core of your Heart, ever so quietly, when no one is watching.

Just you and God know this humbleness, deep within your Heart!

And, I would like to add here, the more humble one becomes, they realize there is less and less reaction to 3D Illusions!!

It is Faith that reminds you, ever so quietly, within the deepest recesses of your Heart that, which created me, will prevail. That which created me will endure the tests of time. That which created me will find me and bring me safely home.

You are NOT ALONE! You have NEVER BEEN ALONE! That is the ILLUSION, THAT YOU SAID YOU WOULD PARTICIPATE IN AND MOVE THROUGH!!

FAITH, my Dear Friends, moves you through the ILLUSION and She is as real as you are. Were you to look upon Her face, you would behold a beauty that words cannot describe. For Her Heart is as Pure as God's Love and She carries the Sacred Vow to assist all Mankind safely Home.

And again I say, Faith PULLS you forward!!

I would greatly encourage you, take time to go within and cultivate your relationship with Faith. She is so very willing to give you thoughts of encouragement, thoughts of hope, and feelings of trust.

In the quietness of your Heart, cultivate a sense of gratitude for Faith. This will bring humbleness within your Being and allow you to feel your Divine Parents as nothing else ever has.

Faith carries a Divine Vibration of Hope, Sincerity and Humbleness.

It is this Divine Vibration of Faith that every student of Spiritual Ascension will need to cultivate. You will come to a point within your Spiritual Journey, where you will recognize that 99% of everything you do comes from a place of Faith.

This is good, My Dear Friends, this is very good!!

This is precisely how you learn to allow the Will of God to manifest in your Life from your Heart of Sacred Fire.

I would like to expand on this. What is meant by the Will of God? For some, I hear fear that God will want me to do this or that, for others I hear fear that God will ask me to take this away or that away from my life.

My Dear Friends, the Will of God does not ask us to do anything that takes away our JOY!

Please remember this, there is no exception.

The Will of God does not take away our JOY. In fact, the Will of God adds and expands our JOY.

🌿 *IF YOU CAN COME TO THE PLACE OF CREATING GOD'S WILL IN YOUR LIFE FROM A SPACE OF JOY, YOU HAVE WON!! And it resides within your Heart of Sacred Fire.*

🌿 *IF YOU CAN COME TO THE PLACE OF CREATING GOD'S WILL IN YOUR LIFE FROM A SPACE OF JOY, YOU HAVE WON!! And it resides within your Heart of Sacred Fire.*

🌿 *IF YOU CAN COME TO THE PLACE OF CREATING GOD'S WILL IN YOUR LIFE FROM A SPACE OF JOY, YOU HAVE WON!! And it resides within your Heart of Sacred Fire.*

It is written. So Be It & So It Is.

It would serve you greatly to read those words above over and over and over.

To create God's Will in your Life in JOY within your Heart of Sacred Fire, is the KEY that pulls everything together.

LEARN TO SET DIVINE INTENTION.

"I set the Divine Intention; God's Will fulfills All My Desires as I move from my Heart of Sacred Fire."

As you vibrate and manifest the Will of God, there are many paths and yet the Will of God is the one that holds Joy, Love and Light.

This is a beautiful surrender to Divine Mind and with it comes a JOY that NO-thing ever created can compare.

The JOY that comes from surrender to God's Will is a JOY that will lift you up, fill your Heart with Hope, and steady your pace to fulfill your Destiny.

In fact, My Dear Friends, there is no other vibration that compares to the JOY of God's Will in your Life.

It is, without a doubt, the Ultimate Space, for you have moved through the Illusion, and stepped in Faith, into the Arms of Mother/Father God Energy.

(There will be times, that you cannot see your hand in front of your face, and yet your Heart tells you to trust that which created you. That is FAITH and She is leading you Home.)

And again I say, Faith PULLS you forward!!

And this is precisely where your SOUL knows you need to be to manifest your Spiritual Ascension.

Think on this for a moment, all leads us back to that which created us! No exception!

It is the fabric that constitutes our Beingness. One cannot deny that which created it!

And everyone, sooner or later, MUST return to their Creator.

For those of you who are drawn to My Energy, Beloved Sanat Kumara, I assure you Mother/Father God is waiting to meet you Now.

Anything to the contrary is the *Illusion.* You said you would participate in that *Illusion. And I said I would come back and remind you NOW, how to move away from the Illusion and manifest the Ascension*

Dimension within your Heart of Sacred Fire.

And JOY of JOYS, I AM Here Now, to remind You, My Dear Friends!!!

The Will of God resides within your Heart of Sacred Fire and holds your Divine Blueprint. **It is in this Sacred Space that every Spiritual Ascension student will learn to Be One with 'I AM'.**

You will learn through experience as you move away from 3D, into 4D and eventually 5D, to say within your Heart:

- *"Guide Me God, Guide Me, Thy Will Be Done on Earth as It Is In Heaven".*
- *"Guide Me God, Guide Me, Thy Will Be Done on Earth as It Is In Heaven".*
- *"Guide Me God, Guide Me, Thy Will Be Done on Earth as It Is In Heaven".*

The very second that you say these words, every cell within your Being resounds the Clarion Call of Celestial JOY, for your Cells know who created You.

And Your Cells have been waiting a long, long time for you to wake up and say,

"Thy Will Be Done Mother/Father God, Thy Will Be Done."

- And it is at that precise second that you ARE in Divine Alignment with Divine Mind.
- And it is at that precise second that Heaven IS created on Earth.
- And it is at that precise second that your Divine Blueprint has stepped forward and you are One with the Great 'I AM'.

> ✍ And it is at that precise second, your
> Diamond Core God Cell manifests your
> Light Body from your Heart of Sacred Fire.
> ✍ And it is at that precise second, you KNOW
> JOY, JOY, JOY!!!!

Learn to FEEL what I have just shared with you. Come to a place of feeling this within your Heart and you have Won!!

My Dear Friends, this is how you cultivate Faith, Hope and Trust, and it is a Journey of Everlasting Joy as you manifest the Will of God, AKA as Heaven on Earth!!

It is written. So Be It and So It Is.

DIVINE BLUEPRINT STEP FORWARD
DIVINE BLUEPRINT STEP FORWARD
DIVINE BLUEPRINT STEP FORWARD and BE, [I AM]

The Eleventh Key

MOTHER GOD/FATHER GOD

A long time ago there was a yearning in the Heart of Mother/Father God.

You understand this yearning was a Divine **Vibration** to expand and express consciousness with Love and Light. Love is the Feminine Aspect of Divine Mind. Light is the Male Aspect of Divine Mind. The Feminine is allowing, receiving, BE-ing. The Masculine is power, giving, wisdom.

(Here, I would like to point out; there are more life streams on this planet that are perfecting the Energy of Allowing, BE-ing, as We usher in 5D on Beloved Terra).

Love is Mother God, Light is Father God and as these two Divine Vibrations become perfectly harmonized and balanced within our Hearts, we are able to embrace the Divine Plan, I AM THAT I AM within Heart of Sacred Fire.

It is within this Holy Vibration of Love & Light, [LIFE], that one understands Divine Mind.

It is a blessed space of awareness that Mother/Father God wants each of us to experience 24/7.

And in this space, we understand At-One-Ment. For here in this Sacred Space of Love & Light, perfectly harmonized, we are Co-Creators with God. This is a glorious privilege freely given and it is your Destiny.

I would like to add here, you will spend Eternity understanding and expressing your unique Divine Vibration within Mother/Father God. For Mother/

Father God is the Great 'I AM' Energy. And OH, what WONDER and JOY await you!!

In fact, My Dear Friends, **"I AM" is THE Exclusive Signature Energy of Mother/Father God.**

- **'I AM' vibrates the numerological value of 5 = FREEDOM**
- **'I' vibrates the numerological value of 9 = COMPLETE**
- **'AM' vibrates the numerological value of 5 = FREEDOM**
- **Together "I AM" MANIFESTS THE VIBRATION OF 'COMPLETE FREEDOM'**

What I have just shared with you IS the Divine Energy of Mother/Father God, and it doesn't get any better!! And you can take that to your Spiritual Bank and allow it to earn interest!!

My Dear Friends, if you have not already thought about this, I would like to personally assure you now, your Spiritual Bank is by far the most important investment you will EVER make in the grand scheme of things.

It may not seem so at times, when your 3D Ego is blasting in your face! Please excuse the pun, and yet, without out a doubt, hands down, there is not, nor will there ever be, anything more important that you will ever invest in, that will bring you more in return, than your personal Spiritual Bank. So, as I speak this to you now, please let this rest in your Heart and think on this many times throughout your day.

What investments have I made in my Spiritual Bank?

This Energy called Love is the glue that keeps everything connected. This Energy called Light motivates Creation to express more of Itself. And because of these two perfectly balanced and harmonized Energies, mankind is remembering all that He/She/It is.

Mother/Father God greatly desires for Creation to expand awareness through this wonderful Union of Love and Light......

As each individual practices with this Energy of Love and Light, they experience an abundance of Divine Vibration within the higher levels of consciousness. Please remember there are many and vast expressions of consciousness.

Not all choose to participate in the Love & Light of Mother God/Father God Energy. It is always a choice, and there is no judgment within Divine Mind. Only experience. And so the journey continues.

- It is this Energy of Love which **allows** the Divine Vibration of Mother God.
- It is this Energy of Light which **manifests** the Divine Vibration of Father God.
- The Two vibrate One as 'I AM', which IS your Heart of Sacred Fire.

And always, there is a vibration. And so the journey continues. Ever expanding, ever widening, and ever deepening within Divine Mind.

And as you experience these higher levels of awareness, it is most beneficial for the student of Spiritual Ascension, to flow with a balanced Energy

of Love and Light, which manifests Divine Vibration. Love from Heart Space, Light from 3rd eye space, both synergistically balanced together within the Holy Altar of Heart of Sacred Fire.

And as you allow Mother/Father God to expand within your Heart of Sacred Fire, you experience the Ascension Dimension.

It is the Love of Mother/Father God that will carry you through the storm. And you will come out of it, tested, through the Fire that does not burn, and you will stand, strong, in the Light and Love that created you.

For those of you who have experienced this, you know that which I speak of, and it comes through a humbleness of Spirit. For those of you who have yet to feel this, My words will bring comfort to you in your hour of need. ***I AM THAT I AM.***

As we choose to move forward in the Love and Light of Mother God/Father God, we understand the Divine Vibration of Balance and Harmony. As we choose expansion, we recognize the Divine Balance of Inner Eye (6th chakra) with Heart (4th chakra) and recognize our FREEDOM to participate in LOVE as we co-create expanded Divine Vibrations with Mother/Father God.

It is very important to move from the Core of Mother/Father God, which is in your Heart of Sacred Fire, your Diamond Core God Cell, and balance this connection with your Inner Eye, 3rd chakra. This Energy is the Ascension Dimension Cord. Please ask for My assistance, and I will help you with this.

This becomes a beautiful, creative flow of energy, vibrationally aligned with Mother God/Father God, Divine Mind. This manifests an energy that sustains you, it feeds you.

Mother God is Allowing, BE-ing and Father God is Wisdom, Power.

As you, the Spiritual Ascension student come to this space of awareness; you will KNOW this is your Diamond Core God Cell. Please get an Inner Feeling on this wave of Divine Mind flowing out from your Heart Space. Mother God Allows, Father God Manifests and together I AM that I AM moves in Holy Matrimony, Be-ing JOY, Be-ing PEACE, Be-ing LOVE which moves mountains. And it comes in color!!

This is precisely why YOU came back; to share this Most Blessed Union of Allowing and Power. All eyes are on you My Dearest Friends and We are here with you to ensure that this comes to pass on Beloved Terra. So Be It and So It Is.

And as you recognize this Divine Balance in Mother/Father God, it vibrates peace which passes all understanding. For you stand in your Heart of Sacred Fire, One with Mother/Father God, connecting with Nature Family and sealing with the Royal Angelic Realm in your 3rd eye Chakra, flowing the Ascension Dimension.

Please get an inner visual on this now. Feel this Unconditional Love Energy moving from your Heart of Sacred Fire, up to your 3rd eye and embrace this Divine Vibration of Love and Light, manifesting the Ascension Dimension Cord.

(You will become aware of Violet Light, the Holy Spirit; Gold Light, the Angelic Realm; Emerald Light, Nature Consciousness, and Crystalline White Light, God Consciousness) And My Ascended Peach Energy will surround you!!

It is LIFE straight from Mother God/Father God and holds everything that you need.

It is your FREEDOM right now. I AM THAT I AM.

DIVINE BLUEPRINT STEP FORWARD
DIVINE BLUEPRINT STEP FORWARD
DIVINE BLUEPRINT STEP FORWARD and BE, [I AM]

The Twelfth Key

VIOLET LIGHT

Mother/Father God has given us THE most, glorious self-help tool for Spiritual Ascension. It is called the "Violet Light", or "Violet Flame". Beloved Ascended Master Saint Germaine brings forth the Violet Flame for mankind, assisted by Archangel Zadkiel.

The Violet Flame is the Holy Spirit and has the Divine Authority and Power to QUALIFY ANY MIS-QUALIFIED ENERGY.

I cannot emphasize enough, the importance of protecting yourself with the Violet Light. This is Divine Alchemy at its Best!!

Think on this for just a moment. Close your eyes, breath into your Heart of Sacred Fire, fan the 3-fold flame, allow your awareness to escalate up the Ascension Dimension Cord through your throat and sealed in your 3rd Eye. There you find the Violet Flame Pyramid, within your Holy Eye, which carries the Divine Mark of Eternal Youthfulness and sacredly manifests the Will of God. Move through the ILLUSION and SEE VIOLET LIGHT, THIS IS THE HOLY SPIRIT, balancing and harmonizing All Energy.

Call on Beloved Saint Germaine. He will greatly assist your awareness of the Violet Flame/Light and how to use this for Qualifying Life.

There will be times, when Energy comes your way that is (Mis)-Qualified and you recognize you did not create it.

Archangel Zadkiel reminds you; DO NOT PERSONALIZE THE ENERGY, UNLESS YOU WANT TO GO THROUGH THE DRAMA!!

It is at that precise second that you remind yourself:
"I am Master of Energy or Energy is Master of me."
This becomes your most advantageous opportunity to create a Cosmic Momentum of Qualified Life for the Collective Consciousness, your SOUL Group and Causal Body.

Think on this. You have numerous opportunities to make a difference.

- You have, throughout your day, many circumstances to master energy.
- You have, throughout your day, many vibrations waiting to be Qualified.
- You have, throughout your day, many opportunities to express Love & Light.

DO NOT PERSONALIZE THE ENERGY, UNLESS YOU WANT TO GO THROUGH THE DRAMA!!

It starts within your Heart of Sacred Fire, where you become Master of Energy and flow the Ascension Dimension Cord.

My Dear Friends, there may be times in your journey, that you will become aware of pinholes in your Aura. I, Beloved Sanat Kumara, would like very much to assist you with this from now on.

Those pinholes in your Energy Field occur throughout your day and they allow your Divine Connection to become taxed. As I bring your awareness to this, you will become more familiar with this, if and when it occurs. It happens being around energies that are not life-giving, not life-supporting. Remember (mis)-qualified energy equals death.

> ✍ **Each day, protect yourself with the Violet Light.**
> ✍ **Each day, always bring your awareness to your Energy Field**
> ✍ **Each day, practice Qualifying Life with the Violet Light.**

If you recognize within your Aura/Energy Field, energies that are not life-giving, call in the Violet Light. (I will use 'Light' and/or 'Flame', to explain the same Energy.)

As you practice this daily, visualize or imagine a Light of Violet Color, and surround yourself with this color. This will seal those pinholes, so that you are once again in Divine Alignment.

Again, I AM reminding you, that which is not seen is more real and powerful than that which is seen with the human eye. Learn to see through the ***Illusion!!***

If you find that the Energy Holes are bigger than you bargained for, call on my Energy and I WILL guide you as to how to proceed, you may need outside assistance to seal Energy Holes. There are some who have brought in from past lives, negative information on a cellular level which can cause Energy Holes in the aura. Do not fret over this information, just KNOW, it can happen and you can use the Violet Light to seal any Energy Holes. Please remember the Violet Light/Violet Flame are one and the same, which is the Holy Spirit.

And I would like to add the Holy Spirit carries the Divine Feminine Energy of Allowing.

It is in the 'Allowing', you as the Spiritual Student, recognize it is important to ALLOW the

Energy to be, and move Forward in Love and Light. Don't get stuck! This is where you REST (BE) in your Heart of Sacred Fire!!

This is your lifetime to move your SOUL Group forward in the Love and Light of Mother/Father God with an evolutionary leap in Light Years of Consciousness for the Highest Good of All. There are many who wait with baited breath in the Ethers while you make decisions. Now, more than any other 'time frame' in history, there are Light workers waiting in the Etheric Realm, to assist.

Please allow me to re-word that last statement for added emphasis.

NOW, more than any other time in the History of Planet Earth, there are more Beings of Love and Light waiting to assist and bring God's Will, than ever before!!!

This is where you become aware of the COSMIC PICTURE!!

This is your grand opportunity to fulfill that which you said you would do.

It starts and stops with each one of your choices. We love you, we adore you and we hold that Sacred Space of Faith that you WILL make choices for Qualifying Life within the natural power of your Heart of Sacred Fire, your Diamond Core God Cell.

Practice Being Present with your Awareness and Use the Violet Light, you will automatically anchor God's Will, flowing the Ascension Dimension, from Heart of Sacred Fire.

DIVINE BLUEPRINT STEP FORWARD
DIVINE BLUEPRINT STEP FORWARD
DIVINE BLUEPRINT STEP FORWARD and BE, [I AM]

The Thirteenth Key

ENERGY

There was a very wise man, who once said, "All Energy already exists, and you cannot create more of it." Albert Einstein was referring to Source Energy. And he was correct. It already IS, one cannot create more, for IT IS.

For the Spiritual Ascension student, the practicality of Energy becomes a fine line of Wisdom. Let Me expand on this.

- It is important, that one understands, Energy already exists. IT IS Source Energy.
- It is important, that one understands, Source Energy has always been.
- It is important, that one understands, before Mother/Father God, Source Energy IS, the Great Isness.
- It is important for one to understand, how they choose to work with Energy. And Energy can be used in multitudinous ways. I assure you My Dear Friends, you are not the only Beings using and working with Energy.
- It is important that one understands, Energy is available to all. It is important that one understands, Energy is used by all in multiple ways.
- It is important that one understands, the use of Energy is not judged by Mother/Father God. All is allowed. All is experience.

- It is important that one understands, there are those that would use Energy for reasons that are not defined as 'LIFE Giving'.
- It is important that one understands, LIFE has not been given to all.
- It is important that one understands, only Mother/Father God gives LIFE
- It is important that one understands, Energy is a multidimensional concept that can be used in various forms.
- ***And it is important that one understands, the Energy of Mother/Father God is 'I AM.' It is written. So Be It and So It Is.***

My Dear Friends, I could write another entire book on Energy, and yet it would not serve the purpose that you are needing as a Spiritual Ascension Student. One could spend many lifetimes and many experiences understanding and experimenting with Energy.

In fact, many have. And for them, books have and will be written.

Please remember, Energy, is the substance of Consciousness.

This book is to guide you, the reader, towards Spiritual Ascension. And for that reason, I am choosing to explain the Energy of [I AM].

Truly, 'I AM' IS the Signature Energy of Mother/Father God, which IS the Energy of Divine Mind.

There are those of you who will read this and this one chapter will wake up within you many Illusions from the past, that have kept you from the Great 'I AM'.

There is only One 'I AM', and IT IS Mother/Father God Energy.

Anything to the contrary is the **Illusion.** This **Illusion** has been allowed. And that is another book, also.

I will explain here, there is Darkness that has been allowed in this experience on Beloved Terra. Your decision at any moment: Light or Dark? Which is it? And are you now ready to balance the Light with Love?

And once again, I will state, it is not necessary to go into this discussion about why the **Illusion** was allowed. (Here, your child-like Faith is necessary!!)

What I am about to say is probably one of the most misunderstood and yet most important spiritual truths that you need to grasp.

> ✒ *That which is not seen, is more powerful than that which is seen with the human eye. YOU MUST LEARN TO SEE THROUGH THE ILLUSION!!*

This is where your FAITH steps in and **surrender** to God's Will in Joy carries you Home.

This is all a part of your Divine Blueprint, and you said you would come back and do this job. This job is not for the faint of heart!!

For those of you who ask "why?" you will not find the answers. For the "whys?" will trip you up faster than anything else. In fact, the "whys?" will keep you from the Ascension Dimension.

> ✒ This job is for those who will follow through.
> ✒ This job is for those who know they MUST take responsibility for their Energy
> ✒ This job is for those who WILL RESPECT ALL, NO MATTER WHAT.

◢ This job is for those that KNOW in their HEARTS, they must finish that which they have started.

◢ This job is for those who choose to follow their desires by creating with Divine Intention from their Heart of Sacred Fire.

◢ This job is for those who WILL QUALIFY LIFE, NO MATTER WHAT.

◢ This job is for those who want their FREEDOM more than anything else.

My Dear Friends, this is the purpose of My book.

And WE, of the Spiritual Hierarchy, are here to assist you. You are not alone!! Remember, the Qualification of Energy is a natural power within your Heart of Sacred Fire. And remember, that which is not seen, is more powerful than that which is seen with the human eye. You can take that to your Spiritual Bank and earn interest!!!!

It is important to add here, 'COLOR'. I now have your full attention!!

Color is a Spiritual Tool that absolutely must not be underestimated. And for those of you who are 'color blind', call on My Energy, I will gladly assist you to remember that which you have forgotten. (Even in the Illusion of color-blind there is color!!)

Color is a marvelous Spiritual Tool; it works on a deep cellular level to bring about harmony and balance.

There is no right way or wrong way to perceive color. Just allow your Angels and Spirit Guides to open you up to the **Divine Vibration within color.** And you WILL find a spiritual depth within your Being that has been missing!!

The Energy of Color manifests a Divine Vibration

that can bring healing, when nothing else will. How Simple!!! How Childlike!!!! How Wonderful!!!!

COLOR, PRACTICE USING YOUR IMAGINATION AND BRING IN A MOST GLORIOUS PEACH LIGHT RIGHT NOW. This is My Energy and I AM blessing you Now, with My Ascended Vibration.

And here, you become aware of the Divine Expanded Perception. You have heard the saying 'Think outside of the box!" I am going to bring your awareness to this spiritual thought.

✑ "THINK AS A COSMIC BEING, FOR THAT IS WHAT YOU ARE"

Please get a hold of THE COSMIC PICTURE and FLOW with it!!

Yes, My Dear Friends, think 'as if' you already are an Ascended Master, for in the eyes of Mother/Father God, you are!!! In this journey of Spiritual Ascension, recognize that your Energy is a most, powerful tool to create with. And you must learn to shift your aware-ness to the Expanded Perspective, the Great Cosmic Picture and allow your God Presence to take over.

Memorize this picture I am painting for you!!

You recognize working with your Energy in your Heart of Sacred Fire flowing the Ascension Dimension Cord, becomes your focal point as you manifest your God Presence 18 inches in front of your Heart!!!

Allow your God Presence to take over, each sec-ond, this is thinking as a Cosmic Being.

And as you allow your Energy to BE, 'I AM', you become the Expanded Viewpoint, resting, allowing, BE-ing, 'I AM'.

At this point, you will recognize, it is more important to BE, instead of Do. And you will have less and less to say!!! And then you are flowing the Ascension Dimension from your Heart of Sacred Fire!!

Meditate on those words, ask for My Assistance, and I will open your Inner Eye as you digest the importance of these words. And become Aware of My Peach Energy!!

So Be It and So It Is.

DIVINE BLUEPRINT STEP FORWARD
DIVINE BLUEPRINT STEP FORWARD
DIVINE BLUEPRINT STEP FORWARD and BE, [I AM]

The Fourteenth Key

THE ROYAL ANGELIC REALM

It is the Will of Mother/Father God for Angels, Nature, and Ascended Masters to assist Humans for the Highest Good of all concerned. It has already been named, **THE GOLDEN AGE OF ENLIGHTENMENT, in which the Lion shall lay down with the Lamb. (Which is another way of stating All will come into Divine Alignment.)**

This is what Mother/Father God intended from the Beginning of SOUL, a Divine Vibration of Right-use-ness, Peace and Joy through Free Will, Choice. This Golden Age will be heralded throughout the History of Histories, as 'Heaven on Earth'.

It is Truth, My Dear Friends and ***She*** will BE a most glorious Haven of Rest. And I assure you, ***Every Knee Shall Bow and Every Tongue shall confess that Mother/Father God is the Holy of Holies, the Great 'I AM'.***

I cannot even begin to describe the vast multitudes that await this most auspicious moment. There is a Divine Movement within the Spiritual Hierarchy that is focused on the greatest outpouring of Unconditional Love & Light that has ever been granted in any dispensation since Divine Mind created SOUL.

The Golden Age of Enlightenment will be the greatest experiment to come from Divine Mind and IT WILL END VICTORIOUS AS 'I AM' IS ESTABLISHED ONCE AND FOR ALL, because of Unconditional Love and Light manifested Divine Vibration within Heart of Sacred Fire.

You can take that to your Spiritual Bank and earn more interest!!

If this sounds like a dream, please go into your Heart Space, breathe into your Heart of Sacred Fire and remember.

This memory is within you, it predicates All, and it IS that which you said you would come here to insure, this most glorious Age of Heaven on Earth.

I AM Beloved Sanat Kumara, and I said I would help you remember.

- Heaven on Earth is your Destiny. And you create it each second you allow Divine Vibration to expand within your Heart of Sacred Fire.
- Heaven on Earth is your Destiny. And you create it each second you allow Divine Vibration to expand within your Heart of Sacred Fire.
- Heaven on Earth is your Destiny. And you create it each second you allow Divine Vibration to expand within your Heart of Sacred Fire.

Remember, gratitude, thankfulness, appreciation given to that which created you, brings ABUNDANT LIFE. This Divine Vibration is held within the Adoration Flame, by Archangel Chamuel and His Twin Flame, Archeia Charity. Call on Them and you will expand your Divine Vibration through Adoration. The Adoration Flame manifests a Divine Alchemy which will transform anything that is not of Divine Vibration. Think on these words that I have just shared. Adoration to That, which created you, manifests a Divine Alchemy. It is this Divine Alchemy that many have searched for, one in particular is known as the Fountain of Youth. Adoration towards your Creator will magnetize Heaven within you, it is ETERNAL LIFE and it just keeps getting better.

You have treasures stored within your Causal Body, your Aura of Life, which has followed you from Day One!! As you practice appreciation towards That which created you, a magnetic reaction takes place within Heart of Sacred Fire, your Diamond Core God Cell, and your treasures become your reality. Practice Adoration towards Mother/Father God and your Heart Will Fill With JOY!!!

It is written. So Be It and So It Is.

My Dear Friends, it is extremely important, this picture that I have just painted for you with words. For in those words that I have just shared, are All of Mother/Father God's Helpers: **The Royal Angelic Realm.** They are most magnificent to behold, this most glorious Host of Heavenly Help that is waiting for you. You are not alone. You were never alone. That was the **Illusion** you said you would work through to process your lessons as you create with Divine Vibration.

When is it done? When YOU SAY IT IS DONE!

And now I hear you say, Sanat you are stepping on my toes again. And I AM here to remind you that if your toes are feeling the pinch, get out of those shoes, LET THEM GO!!!!

You and only you have the right to say who or what will have a hold on your life.

No one person, no one event, no one thought has the right to enter your life, unless you allow it!!! This is the truth, no exceptions and now I am driving home for you what you need to hear.

IT IS UP TO YOU, IT HAS ALWAYS BEEN UP TO YOU, AND IT WILL ALWAYS BE UP TO YOU!!! IT IS YOUR CHOICE!!

Are you ready to allow Heaven to help? You have at your disposal, the most glorious Host of Enlightened Beings, they are your ANGELS OF LIGHT AND LOVE, and they are waiting for your call.

Archangel Michael has Legions at His Right Arm, and if you would like to know how many are in a Legion, let your imagination roll! He has more Angels waiting to manifest God's Will than there are pebbles of sand on your beaches. Think on this, My Dear Friends. Can you imagine how many Angels that is?

It staggers the imagination to think and you would not be able to count in your lifetime how many Angels there are waiting to manifest God's Will. At the risk of repetition, I AM going to repeat that last statement.

You would not be able to count in your lifetime, how many Angels there are right now waiting to manifest the Will of Mother/Father God!!!!

And as you go to sleep tonight, think on that My Dear Friends. You have Legions upon Legions of Glorious Angelic Host waiting to assist, if you will just ask them.

That which is not seen is more real and powerful, than what is seen with the human eye. Learn to see through the Illusion and meet your Angels.

The Royal Angelic Realm serves Mother/Father God from Their Hearts in Love and Joy, and carries Divine Vibration.

I AM giving you an inner visual. This is extremely important. At any second throughout the history of Mother Earth, there were more than enough Angels to manifest God's Glory, it was never in question. The beauty of this is, Mother/Father God has allowed all of you to choose through free will. This is Unconditional Love, pure and without limit.

Within the Great Central Sun, the Holy Altar of Mother/Father God resides, this is a most spectacular picture to behold. Picture, if you will, Legions of Heavenly Host, Seraphim, Archangels, Cherubim all vibrating the Divine Vibration of 'I AM'. This frequency is of such amazing Purity, holding Unconditional Love and Light, and it is most breathtaking to participate as an observer. Within the English Language, there are not enough words to describe the Beauty, Splendor and Joy within the Holy Court of Mother/Father God. Angels serve Mother/Father God from a Heart of Joy. It is their Honor to serve from a Holy Space of Joy. They understand Divine Vibration and wish to expand it also in Love & Light.

"We are all here waiting for you to just ask for our help. We are as close to you as the air you breathe. And we wait with the Greatest Love, to support and guide you."

Just ask, that is all, ask the Royal Angelic Realm. There are more Angels to assist you than the hair on your head, and if you have not hair, then count your breaths, My Dear Friends. For each breath that you breathe, there are 10,000 Legions of Angels waiting to assist you with that next most glorious breath.

As far as your imagination can go, the Royal Angelic Realm exists beyond even that. Think on these words, meditate on them, there are so many Angels waiting to assist you, one cannot even count them. ***And they only know the Will of Mother/Father God. This is their Love of God, to execute Divine Vibration.***

I cannot emphasize enough, how much your life would evolve into Love & Light if you would ask the Royal Angelic Realm to assist you. They do not interfere; they only come into your life when you ask them. They will assist you in Love & Light. Angels never bring fear, only Love & Light. They honor your choices and wish to assist you to manifest Divine Vibration for ABUNDANT LIFE.

Show your appreciation and thankfulness towards the Angelic Realm for their assistance. And you will receive great rewards of Love, Joy, and Light in your life that you had not had before. (Terri would like to share, her Angels crack the walls when they are near her, and this has brought her much joy, as well as validation).

I would also like to add here, Angels appreciate your eagerness!! And by that, I mean they value your expectation of good things coming!! It assists them, to assist you in greater ways.

So bring on the eager expectation and anticipation as you work with your Angels!!

Become childlike in this, trust and they WILL assist you!!! Practice this daily, thanking your Angels for Their Divine Assistance in all areas of your life and you WILL ENJOY ABUNDANT LIFE.

DIVINE BLUEPRINT, STEP FORWARD
DIVINE BLUEPRINT, STEP FORWARD
DIVINE BLUEPRINT, STEP FORWARD and BE, [I AM]

The Fifteenth Key

NATURE FAMILY

It is with great joy, love and honor that I bring forth this information for mankind to remember Nature Consciousness.

I was there when Mother/Father God created Nature Family, I remember well the Joy of Archangel Raphael as Divine Mind manifested Emerald Green Energy of Healing Rays of Light. A Great Momentum of Energy was synchronistically expanded within the Emerald Green Light and from that Light evolved Nature Family.

I AM creating within your Inner Eye a picture of empowerment through Love for *Growth.*

It was that Love for *Growth (Evolution)* that expanded into Nature from Divine Mind.

And Nature has, synchronistically, evolved into many levels, many aspects, and many arenas.

And Nature became Mother/Father God's avenue to bring LIFE into manifestation.

For God understood the importance of 'manifestation' as the Root Races would bring Divine Vibration forward through expansion of LIFE.

And Divine Mind knew *'manifestation'* required an Energy to bring it forward, and God created this 'Energy' known as Nature Consciousness/Family.

Nature Family/Nature Consciousness is responsible for the physical manifestation of your desires. Their job is vast and great. We owe much gratitude and thankfulness to Nature for all that we behold on Mother Earth.

It is Nature that brings Energy into form for mankind's journey on Beloved Terra. (Nature brings 'YOU' into physical form).

Nature only knows the Will of God, and so moves as One with Divine Mind.

It is Nature that works with Higher Self, and the Spirit who chooses incarnation, bringing physical manifestation according to the Highest Good of the individual.

It is Nature that connects you with your Higher Self!! This is why children, animals and people love to be out in Nature!!

So, be certain to include NATURE FAMILY throughout your day, for Nature is your Divine Connection with Higher Self.

(I will walk you through this in My Heart of Sacred Fire meditation.)

Here, again, is another **key,** which is monumental in your Spiritual Ascension.

Nature Family has the ability to assist your spiritual journey.

How childlike! Nature! What do all children love? Nature!!!!!! And why is that? Because children, innately understand, Nature connects them with their Divine Parents. Oh Glory!

How wonderfully simple this becomes for everyone. Mother/Father God created a playground for us All. It is called Nature. I encourage you, everyday, connect with Nature Family. (And, you can take that to your Spiritual Bank and earn interest!!!)

This will quicken your Higher Self and move you on the fast track towards the Ascension Dimension.

You have a plethora of Eternal Growth to choose from. You have Mother Moon, Father Sun and all of your Brothers and Sisters in the Stars.

It is Nature Family that manifests **Growth** on Mother Earth within the vegetable kingdom, the animal kingdom, the mineral kingdom, the insect kingdom and the human kingdom.

It is Nature Consciousness that lovingly provides the Elementals, Devas and Nature Spirits to bring forth the Will of God in form on Mother Earth.

I would like to point out a Spiritual Element that All must come Home to. It is known as 'Self-Worth'. Poems have been written, songs have been sung, and wisdom has come from the Value of 'Self-Worth'. Of all the transformational keys that I have shared with you, it is Nature that shines on your Self-Worth. For it is Nature, my Dear Friends, that created your physical body, in the womb.

And Nature carries the Divine Vibration of Self-Worth. It would serve you well, to ask Nature to show you the Value of Self-Worth.

(Beloved Ascended Master Kuthumi brings forth Nature Consciousness for All to share and understand, and Kuthumi would gladly assist your journey of Self-Worth).

For Nature shines all around you, glowing with Self-Worth, because Nature knows the Love of Mother/Father God.

Please ask Nature to assist you with the Value of Self-Worth. This is most important in your Spiritual Ascension. Self-Worth does not puff one up!!

The Value of Self-Worth lays everything down at your feet that is not of the Love and Light of Mother/Father God Energy. Nature understands this through and through.

Have you watched a storm, my Dear Friends, roll through. And after the storm, have you seen how Nature may look devastated. If you look closely through Divine Expanded Perception, you will see how Nature in All Her Glory lays down before Mother/ Father God in total, complete and humble surrender.

For those of you who know this in your Heart, you will feel tears of Joy fill your eyes, for you know that which I speak of.

And yet, Father Sun comes out again, and Nature, in all Her Glory, rallies round and Co-Creates again with Divine Mind, bringing Eternal Growth for all to behold and enjoy. ***That is the Value of Self-Worth at its BEST.***

Self-Worth has absolutely, nothing to do with the Lower Ego. Self-Worth is key to your Spiritual Ascension, for as you embrace the Value of your Self-Worth, you come home to All That You Are.

This is essential for you to understand, YOU ARE ONE WITH MOTHER/FATHER GOD. And in that Divine Vibration you come Home to yourself. YOU ARE WOR-THY TO STAND AS ONE WITH MOTHER/FATHER GOD, FOR YOU CARRY 'I AM' DIAMOND CORE GOD CELL IN THE CENTER OF YOUR HEART of SACRED FIRE! ANY-THING TO THE CONTRARY IS THE ***ILLUSION!!***

And, my Dear Friends, if there is any-thing that stands between you and your Destiny, ask Nature to assist you in letting it go. And Nature WILL!!!! And please be open as Nature guides you in how to LET GO!

No matter what may come, you are solidly rooted in Divine Mind. Your Value is most graciously sealed, in At-One-Ment with All That Is, the Great I AM!

That is Self-Worth at its BEST, my Dear Friends.

Call on Nature to explain this to you.

And the Birds will sing in your ears, and the grass will grow at your feet, and the sun will shine on your skin, for the Value of Self-Worth is Nature's Song to Humanity.

So Be It and So It Is.

And My Dear Friends, it is Nature that will assist you to manifest your Light Body.

Nature holds the Divine Template of your Electronic Presence in their Crystal Grids.

Through practice of My Heart of Sacred Fire Meditation, Nature will activate the Crystal Grids for manifesting your Light Body, from the Ascension Dimension Cord. (All Crystals Hold Divine Vibration of Mother/Father God)

I would like to talk for a moment about your pets. For those of you who have pets, I know how much love they bring to you. It is important for you to understand this from a Divine Vantage Point. Remember, there is always a vibration. And your pets also, have the experience of vibration, as do you.

If you find a strong emotional attachment to your pet, I would encourage you to go within and meditate on this. Your pet will not move forward in the Love and Light of Mother/Father God if you hold them. I can hear some of you saying; now Sanat, you are stepping on my toes!!! Please excuse My intrusion.

I am speaking for Nature Consciousness when I point out that pets come to Beloved Terra to forward the consciousness of their SOUL Group. And they understand, emotional attachments, can impede their progress. I understand your love for your pets. What you have to understand is coming to a point of

Unconditional Love. In this space, there are no attachments, just allowing.

And once again, I say to you, that which is not seen, is more real and powerful then what is seen with the human eye. Learn to see through the Illusion. ***Your pets have lessons, as do you!!! Meditate on this!!***

I have brought your awareness here for your SOUL Growth. Go within and ask in the quietness of your Heart and you will be guided as to your relationship with your pets.

Make it a point, throughout your day, show gratitude and appreciation to Nature.

Connect with Nature in physical form, be it plant or animal and honor Nature in Spirit form, which includes Fairies, Devas, and Elementals.

And I would like to add here, for those of you who choose to connect Etherically with Nature, you might try calling in the Dragon Realm, and Unicorns.

Most Dragons serve the Love and Light of Mother/Father God and always have. Dragon Energy is Master of all five elements: air, water, earth, fire and ethers. They are the only Being within Nature Family that is Master of all five elements. They can be a great spiritual resource. (Ask Me in meditation and I will assist you with this, if it speaks to your Heart!)

And Unicorns, I do not need to tell you, just ask them!!

DIVINE BLUEPRINT STEP FORWARD
DIVINE BLUEPRINT STEP FORWARD
DIVINE BLUEPRINT STEP FORWARD and BE, [I AM]

HIGHER SELF

Here, within your Heart Space are where your feelings originate. And those feelings that you feel, hold the vibration of SOUL that can set you free. ***Yes, I AM here to tell you now, those FEELINGS THAT YOU FEEL, are KEY to your Freedom.***

Your feelings are the 'speech-patterns' your Higher Self uses to guide you in this journey on Beloved Terra. If you deny your feelings coming from your Heart Space, you deny who and what you are!!

Let us talk about those feelings for a moment.

Perhaps you feel that negativity is something that is holding you back. It might be a recurring theme in your life experience. It might be a person or situation that keeps annoyingly coming up in your life experience. It might be some persistent thought that occurs within your Heart Space, perhaps at times, even surprises you!

Those 'vibrations' (feelings) have come to you as teachers from SOUL. Please remember, your Higher Self is your direct extension of SOUL.

They (feelings) are here to teach you how to become One with Mother/Father God.

Those feelings remind you how to move back into your Heart of Sacred Fire, and LET GO of Lower Ego and REST (BE).

Those vibrations from a recurring theme, those vibrations from a person or situation, those vibrations from thoughts, have all come to teach you how to listen to your Higher Self. You recognize this as 'intuition' or 'gut-feelings'!

The feelings that you feel, tell you either something is amiss or that everything is right in your world. You understand this comparison, for you have surely experienced it before. Emotional pain is experienced and then you identify a vibration.

Emotional Pain is allowed for the benefit of recognizing 'attachment'!!

If you purposely sedate yourself, you are turning your back on that which created you!!!

Please forgive my harsh words and yet I need to drive a point home for you, now. You have spent eons covering up your Heart Space with TRASH!!! It is now time to look within, turn on the faucet, and let those tears flow like a river. I assure you, those precious tears will wash you clean and clear your SOUL. Yes, let those tears flow for all those disappointments, all those hurts, all the pain, let those tears flow, and your Heart will thank you. For in that precise moment that you humble yourself as a child before your Creator, YOU HEAL!!!

And now, SOUL is stepping forward for YOU and is most assuredly presenting you with circumstance after circumstance to look at your feelings and recognize what is the lesson that particular Teacher has come to show you.

DO NOT DENY YOUR FEELINGS!!!

Your biggest enemy is yourself. And your grandest friend, lies within your Heart of Sacred Fire, Your Diamond Core God Cell, 'I AM'.

Make no mistake about this my Beloved Friends, SOUL will not let up on you until you get what it is that you said you needed to get. Yes, My Dear Friends, you have set up test after test with your Higher Self, according to your Divine Blueprint, that which is for your Highest Good.

There is NO-thing outside of you that is testing you. *You are testing you!*

Here I must add, DO NOT COMPARE YOURSELF TO SOMEONE ELSE!

You will not find solace in another person, or their circumstances. This is how you learn to go quietly within your Heart and connect with your God-Presence. Please pay close attention to what I AM saying. **THIS IS PRECISELY HOW YOU LEARN TO GO WITHIN AND CONNECT WITH YOUR GOD-PRESENCE. STOP LOOKING OUTSIDE OF YOURSELF!!!!!**

- Sometimes, My Dear Friends,
  the dots won't connect!!
- Sometimes, My Dear Friends,
  nothing will make sense!!
- Sometimes, My Dear Friends, you will surely feel as if you are on the wrong planet!!
- And Sometimes, My Dear Friends,
  you will feel totally and completely ALONE!

And I hear you say, I can't do this Sanat, it is too hard for me!! And, I AM here to guide you and remind you, lovingly, YES, YOU CAN DO THIS!!!

This is where strength of character is built!!!

I agree, the job is not always easy, in fact, sometimes it seems impossible. And, that is the *Illusion.* For ALL is already in Divine Order. You are learning to move through the *Illusion* and **BE, One with 'I AM'.**

AND WHEN YOU COME TO A SPACE OF LOVING YOUR TEACHER,

THEN – YOUR TEACHER BECOMES HEAVEN FOR YOU!!!!

- *You are not trying to change the Teacher, first you LOVE IT!*
- *And in that LOVE, you Honor that space!*
- *And in that Honoring, You are allowing the Will of God!*
- *And in that Allowing the Will of God, you REST (BE) in your Heart of Sacred Fire!*
- *And as you Rest (BE) in your Heart YOUR TEACHER BECOMES HEAVEN FOR YOU!!!!!*
- *And NOW, You manifest 'I AM' from your Heart of Sacred Fire!!!*

SOUL knows what is for your Highest Good. SOUL WILL keep you to the task until your vibration is 'I AM' One with Mother/Father God.

Sometimes, this takes numerous lifetimes. Have there been times in your life, that you felt a space occurred that you cannot consciously be accountable for it? It was at that precise moment, SOUL was working with you, guiding you to manifest that which is for your Highest Good. You, laughingly call these brain farts! (Please pardon the expression)

My Dear Friends, SOUL is working with you on Cosmic Levels and it creates space on a physical level for that which you cannot account!

Always, SOUL is working with you, and make no mistake about this; SOUL will do what SOUL has to do to manifest your Highest Good, according to the Will of Mother/Father God. (How are you feeding your SOUL?)

Please remember, that which is not seen is more real and powerful than that which is seen with the

Human Eye. You must see through the ***Illusion*** and BE ONE WITH 'I AM'.

As you have learned to live your life in 3D, you are beginning to recognize all of the ***Illusions*** that separate you from the Love and Light of Mother/Father God.

Those ***Illusions*** come to you in the form of teachers.

Yes, My Friends, all of those experiences from 3D ***Illusion*** have taught you well. They are your teachers that you have created. This has been a most glorious experiment upon Beloved Terra.

You said you would come back and either wrap up old karmic debt or help promote the Love and Light of Mother/Father God. Both experiences have come with great sacrifice.

Are you finished with your lessons? Are you finished with 3D? Are you finished with the ILLUSION?

IF YOUR ANSWER IS YES –

- **STEP BACK FROM THE DRAMA & QUALIFY LIFE within your Heart of Sacred Fire**
- **STEP BACK FROM THE DRAMA & QUALIFY LIFE within your Heart of Sacred Fire**
- **STEP BACK FROM THE DRAMA & QUALIFY LIFE within your Heart of Sacred Fire**

This IS becoming Master of Energy, and it is absolutely essential for your Spiritual Ascension.

Qualifying Life affords you THE opportunity to trust your God Presence/Higher Self AND MANIFEST THE ASCENSION DIMENSION from your Heart of Sacred Fire.

This is where you absolutely must flow your Energy within the Ascension Dimension Cord. You

WILL learn to LET GO of Lower Ego Energies!!!

As you trust your Higher Self, you pass all tests and stand in your Heart of Sacred Fire, Master of Energy. Childlike TRUST is FAITH and manifests the Ascension Dimension.

For those of you wanting to move beyond this now, I AM here to tell you, look within your Heart of Sacred Fire, and REST (BE)!!

There is a most Holy place within your Heart. Yes, My Dear Friends, the Arms of Mother/Father God are waiting to hold you and give you a ***PEACE*** that will literally lay everything at your feet. For in the Arms of Mother/Father God, there is only **LOVE**.

There is NO-thing that can vibrate in that Love, except more of the same!!

AND WHEN YOU COME TO A SPACE OF LOVING YOUR TEACHER,

THEN – YOUR TEACHER BECOMES HEAVEN FOR YOU!!!!

It is this Love of Mother/Father God that will set you free. For as you allow this Unconditional Love to flow within your Heart, the Mountains will bow, the Oceans will part and this most glorious planet in all Her dominion will decree the Holiness of the Love that Mother/Father God brings to All. And this happens as you allow the Will of God to move from your Heart of Sacred Fire, flowing the Ascension Dimension.

Imagine this LOVE that heals all wounds, that makes the blind to see, the deaf to hear and the lame to walk. Imagine this Unconditional Love in your Heart, for it is there waiting for you.

I encourage you to meditate on these words that I bring you. There is a Divine Vibration in these

words that will activate your Divine Blueprint and move you towards Healing on all Levels.

(Practice with your Imagination, God's LOVE, this allows Diamond Core God Cell, I AM, to manifest your Light Body) And please do this in Color, allowing my Peach Energy to assist you!!

And so you come to recognize as you move through these experiences that trust in Higher Self, which is your God Presence, (directly from SOUL), becomes vitally important; as you manifest the Ascension Dimension.

This trust translates into faith in action. You learn to listen to your Higher Self, within your Heart of Sacred Fire, and balance this entire action through your 3ʳᵈ eye, flowing the Ascension Dimension Cord.

(In My Heart of Sacred Fire Meditation, I will walk you through this.)

It takes practice and persistency. And it takes **UNDIVIDED ATTENTION!**

Your Heart of Sacred Fire symbolizes Unconditional Love (allowing, BE-ing), the 3ʳᵈ Eye Space symbolizes Light (wisdom, power) and both must be Divinely Balanced. And between the two, your Throat Chakra is allowing you to speak your truth according to the Will of God. I have just explained the Ascension Dimension Cord.

Remember, the Qualification of Energy is a natural power within your Heart of Sacred Fire.

It is in this Divine Balance the individual recognizes a Divine Vibration that is synchronistically balanced with Divine Intention.

Your test, daily, hourly, minute by minute, is to recognize this Divine Balance and create from that balance, with Divine Intention. (It gets easier, the more you practice.)

I AM here to tell you, there is a space between the Heart and the 3ʳᵈ Eye. This space is Mother/ Father God Energy (Ascension Dimension Cord) and it is vibrationally held within your Being by Nature Consciousness. Your ANCHOR is Diamond Core God Cell [I AM]. Please get an inner visual on this now. Mother God is a Silver Cord, Father God is a Gold Cord and Nature Family is an Emerald Cord, all three intertwined and moving up from the Heart of Sacred Fire, through the throat and sealed in the 3ʳᵈ Eye, your Holy Eye. This Divine Pattern resonates Love and Light and holds your Eternal Youthfulness. It would become greatly beneficial to hold this Divine Pattern of Alignment within your consciousness and feel it throughout your day. It is Heart of Sacred Fire, flowing the Ascension Dimension Cord.

Perhaps there are energies that you become aware of that are less than Love & Light. I AM choosing to use words that are life supporting, and it would serve you well to remember your speech techniques!!

The words that you speak can Qualify life or they can (Mis)-Qualify death!!

And so, if you become aware of energies that are not filled with Love & Light, you learn to instantly go to your Divine Pattern (the Ascension Dimension Cord), created between your Heart and 3ʳᵈ Eye.

From there, you test the energies. You WILL know My Dear friends. You WILL be shown what to do and how to proceed. It is here, that I wish to assure you, Mother/Father God has always had a plan for you. It would seem at times, as if, you have been hung out to dry!! I assure you that is not the case!

Your Higher Self is within you at all times!! The separation is the *Illusion!!* And the choice is yours! Do I choose to stay in the Illusion, or do I choose to Go Within my Heart of Sacred Fire, and Rest (BE, I AM)?

Learn to test the energies. If they bring you anything that is not of Divine Vibration, which is Love & Light, they are of the Lower Ego. Don't go there!
Go back into your Heart of Sacred Fire and REST, (BE, I AM), protecting yourself with the Violet Light.

Perhaps there is a block or a hole within your Multi-Dimensional Being from past life experience that needs healing. Your Divine Pattern will guide you as to what to do.

Permanent healing takes place on all levels and is sealed from SOUL all the way to Conscious Level. (I explain Energy Holes in Chapter 12, Violet Light).

Sincerely, call on My Presence, with All Your Heart and I, Sanat Kumara, will guide you as to how to proceed. (My Ascended Energy is Peach Color).

As you move through these pages, my Ascended Vibration will bring your awareness on a conscious level if there are blocks that need to be Qualified or Energy Holes that need Divinely Sealed. As you practice My Heart of Sacred Fire Meditation and these Spiritual Ascension Keys you will be Divinely guided as how to proceed.

Learn to trust in your Divine Pattern of Alignment, housed within your Heart and sealed in your 3rd Eye. This Divine Alignment is the precise replica of SOUL Energy created by Mother/Father God before time began. AKA, the Ascension Dimension Cord.

There will be moments of confusion, doubt and fear. These are all of the Lower Ego. And this is your test, from yourself, to ALLOW HIGHER SELF TO TAKE OVER.

Remember, this is where you get out of your head, and REST IN YOUR HEART OF SACRED FIRE and BE, 'I AM'.

This is practicing trust in your Higher Self. It comes from a Divine Vantage Point.

And you prove this to yourself, each time you let go of the need to control!! It is childlike Trust and Faith, the essence of things hoped for, the evidence of things not yet seen.

(Have you ever looked into the eyes of a child and felt your Heart strings pulled as you recognize their trust in you?)

This child-like trust brings a deep, abiding peacefulness that can only come as you learn to REST (BE, 'I AM)' IN YOUR HEART OF SACRED FIRE.

All Ascended Masters have put these Keys of Spiritual Ascension to the test. No exceptions. **You absolutely must LET GO OF THE NEED TO CONTROL, AND REST (BE, I AM) IN YOUR HEART OF SACRED FIRE.**

And again I say, that which is not seen, is more powerful than that which is seen with the human eye. Learn to see through the *Illusion* and BE, 'I AM' your True Self.

It is written. So Be It and So It Is.

DIVINE BLUEPRINT STEP FORWARD
DIVINE BLUEPRINT STEP FORWARD
DIVINE BLUEPRINT STEP FORWARD and BE [I AM]

The Seventeenth Key

ASCENDED MASTERS

From Divine Mind, LIFE was created. And LIFE has given us so many opportunities to explore. It has been My Divine Intention, that you are understanding how much greater LIFE is than that physical body you are occupying. In fact, My Dear Friends, your physical body is an avenue of expression that in the scheme of things is a fraction of Infinity.

Now, if you could but for a moment, get an inner visual on that description, it would assist Me, as I drive my point home for you!

A fraction of Infinity, think on that!! Your physical body is precious indeed, and yet, a mere shadow, passing in the night, compared to the Cosmic Being that you are. Please grasp the COSMIC PICTURE. This is monumental that you understand what I am pointing out!!

As you look in the mirror, what do you see? You see looking back at you a Holographic ***Illusion.*** You see looking back at you, part and parcel of Source Energy. And, My Dear Friends, you see looking back at you, SOUL, merged with Divine Mind, expressing in 3D.

For those of you who are drawn towards the Ascension Dimension, your awareness should bc projecting a Holographic 'I AM' Presence out in front of you about the same length as your Ascension Dimension Cord. (This would be 18 inches from Heart to 3rd Eye, and also 18 inches out from your Heart Space). This will eventually fill your every waking thought and Virtual Reality is what you are practicing with to manifest your Light Body.

Please call on My Ascended Energy, so that this mental exercise becomes easy for you, second nature, if you will!!

You will become more and more aware of the Crystalline 'I AM Presence' Energetic Templates surrounding your physical body, as you familiarize yourself with this Virtual Reality, projected from your Heart of Sacred Fire, flowing the Ascension Dimension Cord.

Pardon Me, if this seems complicated. Far from it! It is most beneficial for you to understand the Depth of your very Beingness. And Ascended Master is what you are moving towards. And the closer you move towards Ascended Master, the closer you come home to your Freedom, 'I AM that I AM'.

I would like to point out; I am not suggesting that you negate the care of your physical body. It is part of your taking responsibility, to listen to your body's Innate Wisdom on what it needs to excel in total health and well-being. This also holds true for your mental health and spiritual health.

If I could encourage you, it would be to help you let go of 3D Illusion! This is part of the journey, letting go of the if's, and's, what's, how-to's and why's of 3D. Please DO get out of that left-brained thinking that has kept you in the ***ILLUSION***. Once again, you are being asked to move in childlike Trust and let Faith guide you home.

Perhaps, now would be a wonderful time to remind you of your SOUL Agreement. You said you would come back in this time and in this life expression and be a part of this glorious experiment, and FEED YOUR SOUL!!!

I will share this again; Mother Earth is the ONLY planet doing what is being done. She is KNOWN throughout the Universe as the School for the Gods and She represents the Spiritual Aspect of FREEDOM!

And again I say, She is Our Hero!! And Glory Be, that She Is!!

May I share with you, go out at night and find My Home, Beloved Venus, and if you listen very closely with your Inner Ear, you will hear a Song of JOY We sing for Beloved Terra, Our Love for Her knows no boundaries!!

You are the Gods, my Dear Friends, and you agreed to participate in 3D Illusion, through Choice and Free Will, manifesting your Electronic Light Presence, I AM that I AM.

Oh, what a journey this has been!!

And, I, Beloved Sanat Kumara, along with the Royal Angelic Realm, Nature Family, the Great White Brotherhood and the Spiritual Hierarchy would like to state emphatically NOW, hold onto your hats!!!

The Ride is getting better and better, and all eyes are on you! No pressure! (Please excuse the pun). Just wanted to assist you on an inner visual here!

Multitudes (Way Past the Millions) are watching YOU, My Dear Friends, as you move from 3D to 5D. And, THEY are learning right along with you. Divine Mind is expanding as you expand! SOUL is evolving as you evolve!

And Source Energy is always waiting for you!!!

And so, *Ascended Masters* is what you are Becoming!

And I assure you, my Dear Friends; it is a Journey into INFINITY!!!

- **Ascended Masters are Master of Energy, through Qualified LIFE**
- **Ascended Masters only know the Will of God**
- **Ascended Masters only work with Divine Vibration**
- **Ascended Masters totally vibrate Unconditional Love**
- **Ascended Masters rest (BE) in their Heart of Sacred Fire, flowing the Ascension Dimension**
- **Ascended Masters know NOW is All There IS**
- **Ascended Masters Co-Create with Divine Mind**
- **Ascended Masters embrace the Journey of LIFE, as 'I AM'**
- **Ascended Masters have earned the privilege of their Electronic Light Presence**

I would like to clarify for you; the Higher Dimensions beyond 5D are waiting for those who choose to embrace them. It is known as 'Infinity' and to move into the Higher Dimensions as an Ascended Master, glorifying the Love and Light of Mother/Father God is, without a doubt, a Sacred Honor and Privilege. And I do look forward to sharing this Higher Dimension journey with you!! Take that to your Spiritual Bank and I will be there to compound your interest!! You have my word on that!!

So Be It and So It Is!!!

You are reading this book, because SOUL has put it into your hands. You are drawn to My Energy, Beloved Sanat Kumara, because I said I would come back and remind you of your Divine Blueprint.

You are right now, working with your Cosmic Beingness every night that you sleep, preparing for THE Cosmic Moment on Beloved Terra. A moment that will resound throughout the Universe, a most glorious moment, indeed!!

AND IT WILL BE KNOWN AS THE ASCENSION DIMENSION!!

For in THE ASCENSION DIMENSION moment, heralded as the **Golden Age of Enlightenment,** every knee shall bow, and every tongue shall confess that Mother/Father God is the Great I AM, and All Ascended Masters, will gather round as will the Royal Angelic Realm, Nature Family, Galactic Light workers and the Spiritual Hierarchy.

This is what All are moving towards, Ascended and Free!!

Think on this, my Dear Friends. If this speaks in your Heart, then Ascension Dimension is for you!! Don't delay!! Go within and ask, in the quietness of your Heart.

Ask and you will hear much Love and Joy.

For your Heart of Sacred Fire is the Holy Temple of 'I AM'.

I have prepared this book according to the Will of God, knowing these words would wake up those that needed to wake up. And My words carry a Divine Vibration which your Heart of Sacred Fire knows is Truth!

Within each chapter, much spiritual information resides. You will find as you read this book, you will discover something new, each time. For this book is written from Divine Mind and carries the Divine

Vibration of your Electronic Light Presence Template. This is what your SOUL has been waiting for.

And again I say, that which is not seen is more real and powerful than that which is seen with the Human Eye. Learn to see through the Illusion!!!

The Ascended Master earns the privilege of manifesting their Electronic Light Presence.

DIVINE BLUEPRINT STEP FORWARD
DIVINE BLUEPRINT STEP FORWARD
DIVINE BLUEPRINT STEP FORWARD and BE, [I AM]

The Eighteenth Key

ELECTRONIC LIGHT PRESENCE

My Beloved Friends, your ***Light Body*** is more real than your physical body. Please remember, that which is not seen is more real and powerful than what is seen with the human eye. Learn to see beyond the ***Illusion!!***

Your physical body is an expression of Energy that has allowed you to wrap up old karmic debts, balance (Mis)-Qualified Energy for your SOUL Group, and/or assist in the Collective Consciousness as Beloved Terra makes her Ascension to the Fifth Dimension.

Your Light Body is THE manifestation of Divine Vibration of your SOUL, and as you bring together all parts of your experience into a unified whole within Heart of Sacred Fire, you allow SOUL (I AM) to reign supreme as balanced Male/Female Divine Energy, One with Mother/Father God.

As this occurs, your Light Body becomes totally activated, unlimited, eternal, glorifying Mother/Father God, Divine Vibration of Love & Light, and NOW you are flowing the Ascension Dimension.

Light Body, Adam Kadmon, Merkabah, Electronic Presence, these are terms that define your Divine Vehicle that Mother/Father God gifted us, from the Beginning of Creation.

Your ***Electronic Presence*** holds the Unlimited Perfection of Divine Mind and has the capacity to move inter-dimensionally.

And Mother/Father God greatly desires we use this capability to its fullest potential. This is your destiny to become Co-Creators with God in perfect balance of Love and Light, moving as One with Divine Mind.

It is in your Light Body that Divine Vibration resonates unlimited possibilities within Source Energy.

And your Divine Blueprint, the matrix fabric that is your Diamond Core God Cell, housed within your Heart Space on the Holy Altar of Sacred Fire, becomes activated each time you resonate the Love & Light of Mother/Father God Energy.

This Holy Matrix resonates the Energy of LIFE that only Mother/Father God can give. It has been pursued through countless generations, this thing called *Eternal Life,* and yet it is freely given by Mother/Father God in LOVE, without judgment, unconditional and absolute!

This precious LIFE experience that Mother/ Father God has blessed us with is the glorious union of Love and Light manifested in Light Body.

Light Body is your Destiny and anything less is the *Illusion.*

It would serve you well to read the above paragraphs over and over. Much information is contained there, which will assist you in manifesting the Ascension Dimension from your Heart of Sacred Fire. I encourage you to call on My Ascended Energy and I WILL assist you.

Your Light Body is a privilege!! It is a privilege that you will become proficient with Divine Vibration, flowing as an Ascended Master, the Ascension Dimension. Once again, My Dear Friends, I encourage you to call upon My Ascended Energy. I will be able to assist you, as you learn to flow the Ascension Dimension.

And I will also bring to your awareness, that

which is of the Illusion, so that you may LET IT GO!!!! You must LET GO of emotional attachments, they are of the Lower Ego!

Please remember, as long as you are holding on, you are not in a receiving (BE-ing) mode, you are practicing attachment instead of ALLOWING!!

It is Nature that will assist you to manifest your Light Body, 24/7.

Nature holds the Divine Template of your Electronic Presence in their Crystal Grids, which are housed Etherically around you, and strategically placed inside and outside of Mother Earth, also.

As you proceed forward in your Light and Love Evolution, I will guide you to project a Virtual Reality from your Heart of Sacred Fire, flowing the Ascension Dimension Cord. This projection will sit in front of your physical body, about 18 inches out, and will resonate your 'I AM' Presence.

You will literally be able to envision your Light Body in front of you, projected from your Ascension Dimension Cord. The more that you practice this mini-meditation, the more Nature, and your God Presence will activate your Divine Template,

'I AM THAT I AM'.

Please remember, this will only come from a Heart of Unconditional Love and the Ascension Dimension Cord, anchored between your Heart of Sacred Fire and your 3rd Eye.

This also, is the Virtual Reality that all Ascended Masters become proficient with for manifestation.

And once again, I remind you, this is only shown to those who move purely from a Heart of Unconditional Love.

You will be put through the Fire that does not burn, and those that come out of this Sacred Fire, have proven their Love and Devotion to That which created them.

Through practice of My Heart of Sacred Fire meditation, Nature will activate the Crystal Grids for manifesting your Light Body.

As you yearn to consciously connect with your Ascension Dimension Cord, you will learn to activate the Divine Template of your Electronic Light Presence. Close your eyes now, My Beloved Friends, become aware of My Peach Energy, and feel the activation of your 'I AM' Template, flowing between your Heart of Sacred Fire and 3rd eye, your Ascension Dimension Cord. And now become aware of your Merkabah, your Light Field which spherically surrounds you, rotating slowly, connecting the Crystalline Grid Electronic Presence Template. And now become aware of 'I AM' points of Light, Crystalline White Light, pulsating Rays of Unconditional Love, through your Sacred Geometric Field, this all takes place within your Evolutionary Circle, HEART OF SACRED FIRE, EMCOMPASSING THE WIDESPREAD LENGTH OF YOUR ARMS, STRETCHED OUT FROM YOUR SHOULDERS.

This Ascension Dimension Cord that flows, up from your Heart Space to your 3rd eye, holds the frequency of your Electronic Presence and as you manifest this each day, this Divine

Vibration Qualifies old, (Mis)-Qualified energy in your LIFE all the way to SOUL.

Herein lies the beauty of Mother/Father God's Divine Plan for all LIFE.

- Electronic Presence, begin in your Heart Space, allow My Peach Energy.
- Using your imagination, taking a deep breath, fan that Sacred Fire in your Heart.
- Imagine your Ascension Dimension Cord, moving up to your 3rd eye.
- Feel LIFE QUALIFIED from this Holy Dimension
- You transform yourself and your world, each time you practice projecting your Virtual 'I AM' Presence (housed within Diamond Core God Cell), in front of you, from Heart of Sacred Fire, and 3rd eye, flowing your Ascension Dimension Cord.
  (Nature is ready to assist with the Crystal Grid Activation!! Just Ask!!)

This is absolutely, a most loving journey of remembering All That You Are.

And it starts within your Heart of Sacred Fire. And always there is a vibration.

Which vibration do you choose my Beloved Friends?

This is your free-will journey and you said 'choice' would provide you with the grandest opportunities to Co-Create in the Love & Light of Mother/Father God.

I encourage you to practice those five steps until you have it memorized, for this will bring transformation for anything in your life that needs to become a Divine Vibration through Qualified LIFE.

Only those who practice Unconditional Love from their Heart Space and flow the Ascension Dimension Cord, manifesting within The Sacred Fire, will be rewarded their Light Bodies. Remember, this is QUALIFYING LIFE, through your vibration.

This is a Glorious Privilege given to those who Master Energy with Divine Vibration. Remember, Set with Divine Intention and Qualify Life with HEART OF SACRED FIRE.

This takes practice, and through patience and practice you *can* activate your Light Body.

Each time it is activated, the 3D *Illusion* falls away and you become more and more aware of your Divine Blueprint and Shamballa will become visible to the Human Eye.

It is here I would like to ask you to make a date with Destiny.

On November 11, 2011, which is 11/11/2011 which in numerology is 8 (abundance), I would like to invite you to meet Me at the Golden Gate Portal, which is My Etheric Retreat over the Gobi Desert, SHAMBALLA.

This is THE Portal that will Herald the Golden Age of Enlightenment, in which the Royal Angelic Realm, Nature Consciousness and All Galactic Light workers who serve the Love and Light of Mother/Father God Energy will meet. I, Sanat Kumara will be there to usher in the Adam Kadmon Light Body. I will be joined by the other SIX Kumaras of Light and We Will ANCHOR ONCE AND FOR ALL MOTHER/FATHER GOD'S WILL ON BELOVED TERRA. The Lion shall lay down with the Lamb, think on this My Dear Friends, this speaks metaphorically of all the Illusions that you have experienced for eons. The Lion shall lay down with the Lamb and together HEAVEN WILL REIGN ON MOTHER EARTH. I ask you now; will you meet Me at the Golden Gate Portal? I will be there ready to take you in My Arms and Together We Shall Glorify our Creator.

You have my Word on that. I AM SANAT KUMARA. It is Written. So Be It and So It Is.

(NOTE TO READER: Please do not concern yourself over the physical logistics of meeting me there. The Shamballa Train is moving forward and I assure you, if it is for your Highest Good, you WILL be on it!!)

DIVINE BLUEPRINT STEP FORWARD
DIVINE BLUEPRINT STEP FORWARD
DIVINE BLUEPRINT STEP FORWARD and BE, [I AM]

HEART OF SACRED FIRE
Meditation

Let us create now within our Heart Space a beautiful awareness of Mother/Father God.

This is Source Energy at its most spectacular awareness. For here in your Heart Space is that most glorious union of male/female aspects, it is your Diamond Core God Cell; I AM which holds your Divine Blueprint. There, most precious DIVINE FIRE energy expands into a 3-fold flame within your Heart Space. This spark has burned eternally since you moved from SOUL and began your journey.

It is here that one learns to move from and connect with their 3rd eye, (6th chakra) and flow the Ascension Dimension Cord. *As one learns to move from their Heart of Sacred Fire, and flow the Ascension Dimension Cord, they will recognize a discernment that keeps them One with All That Is.*

My dear brothers and sisters of the Light, the Keys to your Self-Mastery are in your Heart Space, your Diamond Core God Cell, I AM, within The Sacred Fire.

It IS the Sacred Fire, which vibrates the Energy of Mother/Father God and it is here that one learns to discern and move from this space. *It is a space of Unconditional Love and it is HERE that you WILL recognize your Divine Nature, your True Essence, I AM that I AM. Again, I SAY, MOVE FROM THE SACRED FIRE!!!!*

It is here that one understands there is no ***Illusion.*** Just pure, Unconditional LOVE, flowing, never-ending, renewing. It is a RIVER of LIFE that flows from your Heart Space and it is Mother/Father God Energy.

> ⚡ **You are an extension of that which created you.**
> ⚡ **You are an extension of that which created you.**
> ⚡ **You are an extension of that which created you.**

And your Diamond Core God Cell, I AM, holds your Divine Blueprint, THE information which will manifest your Electronic Light Body. ***This information will be given freely, as the individual recognizes He/She must move from their Heart Space, a Space of Unconditional LOVE, The Sacred Fire.***

No matter what the circumstances, no matter what has occurred, no matter what is going on around you; at any given moment, ask yourself this question? Am I moving from my Heart Space? And you WILL know the answer instantly. If you are moving from your Heart Space, which IS Unconditional LOVE, YOU WILL BE GIVEN THE KEYS of ASCENSION DIMENSION, IN YOUR PHYSICAL BODY.

I AM SANAT KUMARA, and I AM here to tell you this, there is NO-thing on this planet or on any planet, or in any galaxy, nor within the Universe that will separate you from the Love of Mother/Father God, once you recognize how to stand in your Heart of Sacred Fire.

There is no circumstance, that Mother/Father God is not aware of every hair on your head. And no matter how dark your hour may be, Mother/Father God is as close to you as the air you breathe. REST (BE) in this wisdom!!

God is in your Heart! Always has been, Always will BE!! No exceptions. Anything that has told you different was the ***ILLUSION.***

Mother/Father God wants for you to move forward in the Love and Light of All That Is and claim your Divine Birthright as an Ascended Master.

As you practice 'Heart of Sacred Fire Meditation', you will receive the Divine Vibration of Angels, Nature & Ascended Masters. This will greatly aid your journey of moving through the *Illusion,* manifesting Heaven on Mother Earth, as you flow the Ascension Dimension. And it starts or stops with each one of you!!

Sanat Kumara
Heart of Sacred Fire Meditation

Please take your awareness to your 'Holy Eye' (6th chakra) and with your intention create a most Sacred Space in your Hearts, breathing in My Ascended Peach Energy.

As you breath into your Heart Space, visualize with your 'Holy Eye' a 3-fold flame.

On your left side is the Blue flame (Divine Masculine) and on your right side is the Pink flame (Divine Feminine), and in the center of this flame is your Electronic Presence, again breathing in My Ascended Peach Energy as you stand in the center.

And from this Sacred Fire, emanate concentric, fig-ure eight circles of Alpha/Omega Energy. They are Gold Circles of Light. (Representing Unconditional Love & Light)

And perceive these figure eight Rings of Light, going up from your Heart Space, through your Crown chakra, connecting with your Higher Self.

From there, these never-ending Alpha/Omega fig-ure eight Rings of Light, return down, all the way down your physical body, grounding you to Mother Earth's Crystalline Energy and come up again to your Heart Space.

And now, within your Heart of Sacred Fire, declare your Divine Intention you are the Perfect Creation, manifesting Diamond Core God Cell, I AM THAT I AM.

And, from your Heart Space follow the Ascension Dimension Cord of Three vines, Mother God (Silver), Father God (Gold), and Nature Consciousness (Emerald). All three wrap around each other.

Allow that ***Sacred Ascension Dimension Cord*** to move up from your Heart, through your Throat and seal in your 3rd eye.

AND ACCORDING TO THE WILL OF MOTHER/ FATHER GOD, MY ASCENDED PEACH ENERGY, MANI- FESTS A PEACH CORD ASSISTING YOU ON ALL LEVELS, WE MEET IN THE SACRED FIRE, WE MOVE AROUND BELOVED TERRA AT YOUR THROAT, AND WE SEAL TOGETHER IN YOUR THIRD EYE.

(This is the Portal you are seeing on the front cover of this book.)

This manifests your Divine Alignment with SOUL Energy, housed within your physical body.

Within your 3rd eye and within your Heart, each space holds a Virtual Violet Pyramid, symbolizing the Holy Spirit, and representative of Divine Mind and Divine Heart, Love & Light as One.

- The Violet Pyramid represents the Triune Power of Divine Mind.
- The Violet Light (Holy Spirit) represents the transmutation of (Mis)-Qualified energy and Qualifies it once again to return to Source Energy.

And now, we ask Nature Consciousness to activate the Crystal Grid Matrix, which houses your Electronic Light Presence, I AM, Template.

From North, South, East and West, Nature Consciousness surrounds you with THE Crystalline GRID White Light TEMPLATES OF 'I AM', and as you look closer, you will see on each Ray multitudes of Angelic Fairies manifesting Gods Will for your Highest Good. Dolphin Energy surrounds you now bringing the Eternal Awareness of the Illusion melting away into Violet Light. Become aware of Divine Waves of Love & Light emanating out from your Diamond Core God Cell in your Heart.

SOUL Group Energy moves in, solidifying 'I AM' Presence, glorifying Mother/Father God.

Become aware of your God Presence (Higher Self), gloriously hovering over you, and NOW YOUR GOD PRESENCE MOVES down into your Crown Chakra, moving down through your 3rd Eye, down through your throat and anchoring within your Heart of Sacred Fire, solidifying your Perfection on all levels within your Diamond Core God Cell.

AND NOW, SACRED FIRE HOLDS YOU, PURIFYING YOU WITH THE HOLY FIRE THAT DOES NOT BURN, AND HERE YOU STAND ASCENDED & FREE. AND WITHIN THE SACRED FIRE YOU RECOGNIZE, I AM THAT I AM!

And here you will get an Inner Visual as you manifest from your Ascension Dimension Cord, your Ascended 'I AM' Presence, holographically projected in front of you, about 18 inches. You will become aware of Crystalline White Energy, pulsating rays of Light, coming from your 3rd eye and your Heart, pinpointing perfectly together as 'I AM', in front of you.

If you look closely, you will become familiar with your God Presence standing in front of you, in

this Virtual Reality. Your God Presence is YOU IN PERFECTION, HOLY, ONE WITH MOTHER/FATHER GOD. SO LET YOUR IMAGINATION ROLL, AS YOU ARE PRACTICING THIS, AND YOU WILL BECOME ACCUSTOMED TO YOUR GOD PRESENCE STANDING IN FRONT OF YOU. This is THE Divine Alchemy of the Ascension Dimension you are being privileged to witness. I AM SANAT KUMARA and I surround you NOW with my Ascended Peach Energy, assisting you to embrace your Cosmic Beingness, I AM THAT I AM.

It is Written. So Be It and So It Is.

Please practice this meditation until you have it memorized. As you become familiar with this, it will resonate within your Heart and stir within you a longing to BE, One with Mother/Father God. And that is why I share this with you.

Part Two

GROUP SESSIONS

THE TEACHINGS OF SANAT KUMARA
(Dialoged through Terri Love)

The reader of these group dialogs will receive the healing **Vibration of LOVE from Sanat Kumara,** and as you set an intention of healing, Sanat Kumara will honor that for you, working with your SOUL, for your Highest Good.

So Be It and So It Is.

OCTOBER 16, 2006

Greetings, I honor you tonight as you have come to share your energy with Me. My name is Sanat Kumara, I am most joyous this evening as I step forward through Terri.

I thank each one of you who have journeyed to me tonight, and I will gift you with My Vibration of Love. I bring to you a most, joyous sincere Energy of Mother/Father God Love. And I gift each one of you with this Energy. I am going to surround you with My Awareness around each one of you. It is most sincere, that I ask you to be aware of your Heart Space as you listen to Me share with you.

I love each one of you with a Love that goes beyond all boundaries. It is hard to express in the English Language. When you leave, you will be extremely aware of a Vibration of Love that you have not been able to experience in your Evolutionary Process until now.

(NOTE TO READER: I AM Sanat Kumara, and if this message of Love speaks to your Heart, call on Me and I will assist you to experience this.)

There are no mistakes, I guide each person who comes to hear Me dialog through Terri.

Each one of you has worked with Me, another time, another place. My Energy goes beyond this Time Frame of Mother Earth. I assure you I love this Beloved Star most gloriously. I have held Her in a vision of Love for 'great length of time' that you know in your 3D. I have loved Beloved Terra, beyond even your awareness. She is a Star that Mother/Father God created a long time ago.

And I held Her in My Vision a long time ago. There were many that stepped forward with Me to assist Her, not to fall off Her axis. She reached a point in Her evolution, when She was approaching darkness. It was with great Love that I stepped forward and held Her in a Vision in the Etheric Realm.

I have a Temple, a Retreat over the Gobi Desert. It is called Shamballa. And it resembles my Retreat where I reside on Venus. My Twin Flame is Lady Venus. She stands in this room with us. Whenever you are aware of a Peach Colored Energy, this is I, Sanat Kumara. That happens to be My favorite color in the Ascension Process.

I prefer the Peach Energy. It is an Energy that brings in a Dimension that exceeds the knowledge that is in this room. It is a Wisdom that comes in with Peach Energy. And I would love it if you would learn to work with this color Peach. It would assist you on your Ascension Process, if that speaks to you. I work with groups who are moving forward in the Ascension Process.

It is My Honor to bring the Awareness to all those people who approach Me, and want to understand more about the Ascension Process. It is Terri's wish to make her Ascension Process, I have spoken with her, numerous times, about the Birth and Death process, and she knows this is something she wants to accomplish in this lifetime, the Ascension Process.

I would like to make it very clear, when one moves forward in this Ascension Process, it is not a Be All-End All Theme, that one has reached an Evolution that there is no more.

I, Sanat Kumara, Am continuously evolving in the Love and Light of Mother/Father God Energy. As I bring your awareness there, when one chooses to participate in the Ascension Process, it is a Dimensional Leap that they are making, so they can learn how to connect with their Light Bodies, their Merkabah. Also referred to Adam Kadmon Light Body.

When the person chooses to move beyond Birth and Death, they choose to move into their Light Bodies. You all have your Light Bodies surrounding you; it is called your Merkabah. It was spoken of in "The Keys of Enoch" by one of my wonderful Brothers, Metatron. He wrote the book. He understands the Keys of Enoch, He wrote about the Merkabah, the Adam Kadmon Light Body. It is within your Divine Blueprint and it is in you on a cellular level. It is your choice, if you choose to connect with your Light Bodies in this lifetime.

There is no right or wrong way to approach this. It is always by choice that each person makes a decision throughout their day, a person decides, do they want to keep repeating what they have always been repeating or do they want to shift that energy and bring in an energy that shines a light on that vibration. And the person decides they want to move in a vibrational level that brings them more light. And of course the complement to Light, in the spiritual scheme of things, is Love.

You have Two beautiful Energies, Light and Love. This is Mother/Father God Energy and it resides within your Heart Space. You are created by Mother/Father God Energy.

Your Divine Cell, your God Cell resides in your Heart Chakra. Your Divine Blueprint is within this God Cell, in your Heart Space.

It is your choice, throughout your day, how you choose to connect with this God Cell.

(NOTE TO READER: Divine Cell, God Cell IS Diamond Core God Cell)

I will continuously throughout all of my sessions through Terri, bring the awareness to the Heart Chakra. For it is here that you will find your Key to your Light Body. It is right here (Terri is pointing to her Heart).

I AM Sanat Kumara, and there was a day, in My

evolution, that I was exactly where you are. I understand 3D, I have been there, and I have done it!! I reached a point in My Process; I recognized I needed to connect with My Creator. I was tired of doing 3D. I had done it enough!

I did not choose to re-incarnate, as all of you have done, numerous times. I chose to bring my re-incarnations to a bare minimum.

I AM of the First Root Race, I AM of the Adam Kadmon Creation and I have worked with Metatron on this. And I AM choosing now to bring My Energy back to Beloved Terra. It is My joyous pleasure to bring My Energy and share it on Beloved Terra!!

I choose to bring My Energy now upon Her Beloved Planet, for She needs Us. It is Her turn to make Her Evolutionary Leap. She is already resonating the 5th Dimensional Level.

Even though we understand 3D, 5th Dimension is here right beside you. It is with the left side of the brain, hard to comprehend. This is why I always share with everyone, if you could come back to the Heart Space, we will do this in the mini-meditation for you to understand coming from your Heart Space. If you could connect with this Heart Space and stay here, more often, if you could consciously move from this Heart Space, you would become more aware of 5D, more and more aware of your Light Body. It surrounds you now. It is within you, it is around you, and it is as real as your physical presence. It is just an awareness. It is just an awareness. Moving your awareness to a 5D expression.

It sounds very simple, and yet I hear you express through out your day, you have this circumstance in your life and you have that circumstance in your life. And it is hard for me to stay in my Heart Space. I understand.

Once again, I will share with you; I have also gone

through what you are going through.

IT WAS BECAUSE OF MY PASSION FOR MOTHER/FATHER GOD THAT I CREATED MY LIGHT BODY AROUND ME, AND MOVED BEYOND THE BIRTH AND DEATH CYCLE, AND PROCEEDED TO MOVE INTO THE ASCENDED STATE.

There is a grand adventure waiting for all of you on Mother Earth. The Mayan Calendar comes in with the Energy of 2012, there is much that will transpire upon Mother Earth's back between now and 2012. Even though 2012 (and I AM going to play with you) is already happening!!!!

This is where you get into the Quantum Physics, and I AM not here to confuse you!!

I AM here to Love you. I AM here to bring a Vibration to your Heart that will wake you up! And when you leave here, I AM going to follow you home tonight, and rest with you in the sleep state, and I will whisper in your ears, and I will bring SOUL to you. And I will whisper in your Hearts that you will want to connect with Mother/Father God Energy, it will speak in your Hearts and you will say, *"I have to re-connect with Mother/Father God, for this is what has created me, and this is what I need to return to."*

I want to share with you, there is much to be excited about on Mother Earth, there is much coming into play, and there are many of you that will choose to vibrate your Light Bodies. Once you understand how to do this on a level of 24/7, you understand your Light Body is here for you and you learn to stay in that connected state constantly, you will understand what God meant when God gave you eternal youthfulness, for it is already yours. You will understand what it is when God says, **"My Bounty knows NO limits."** For you will learn to hold your hands out and create what you want.

With that comes great responsibility. God will not give this gift, until each individual understands how to move from their Heart Space in pure Unconditional Love.

It is Love that will guide you into your Light Bodies. Pure Unconditional Love is Mother/Father God Energy. This IS the Energy that will take you into your Light Bodies. And it is the Energy that will give you unlimited possibilities.

You will, in that instant, be able to create whatever it is you choose to create.

You will understand what it is to be a Co-Creator with Mother/Father God Energy.

With that responsibility, that individual will have proved to Mother/Father God, they are ready to move into 5D, in Unconditional Love. They will move only from that Space in their Hearts. It is a Space of Service to Mother/Father God, and it is a Space of ***Surrender.***

It is an interesting Space to learn to move from in your Hearts, and yet, the reward is grander and greater than anything you have ever experienced in any lifetime.

This IS the lifetime that you said you would express and experience!! As I look at each SOUL Group Energy that stands in this room, each one of you have the ability to make your Ascension in this lifetime. It is up to you, if you choose to proceed forward with this. The choice is always yours, anytime. I AM bringing your awareness there, because this is MY job that I said I would do for you!

(NOTE TO READER: I AM Sanat Kumara, and if this information resonates in your Heart, you TOO have the ability to make your Ascension in this lifetime. Call on My Energy and I will assist you with great JOY!!)

I am also bringing the awareness of your SOUL Energy. You have much to pull from.

It is a pool of Energy and it surrounds you, it is called SOUL. It is what you have come from, and it is what you are returning to. I encourage you to learn more about your SOUL Group Energy. This is an Energy that will assist you throughout your day in a manner that would greatly benefit you in your spiritual journey.

It would greatly assist you to move through 3D and connect with Mother/Father God Energy faster. This is the name of the game, for it is a quickening that is upon Mother Earth's Back. It is for all of you to recognize and understand, Mother/Father God is moving upon the back of Beloved Terra.

The day will come, that everyone that said they would walk with Mother/Father God, there will not be a dry eye on this Planet, when the time comes for Mother Earth to be acknowledged as the Shining Star She Is, a most precious Star. She is a Star that is watched by Galaxies upon Galaxies, all eyes are on Beloved Terra.

There has been a grand experiment going on here, it is called the Ascension Experiment.

It has never been done before, what is being done here upon Her back. What She has given to All of Us, is more than I can possibly express in this time frame. Let it suffice to say, I Beloved Sanat Kumara, am sharing with you, Terra has given of Her Heart, Unconditionally for Eons. It is time for Us to assist Her in Her Ascension Process.

If I could encourage you, each one of you, throughout your week, if you could remember when you wake up in the morning, and your feet touch the floor, please connect with Beloved Terra, let your feet touch the ground, and instantly say, I love you Mother Earth. Learn to work with this Energy of Mother Earth, it is called Nature. And Nature is a most precious Consciousness. Nature holds

Mother Earth up, Nature embraces Mother Earth, and Nature happens to be the Children of Mother Earth. They are Her precious Children, and they know nothing but the Will of Mother/Father God Energy.

Work with Nature, work with the Angelic Realm, for They would greatly love to assist you in your Evolutionary Process.

Take in a very deep breath, into your Heart Space, Imagine you are expanding that Heart Chakra. Open that Heart Chakra up, and become aware of, the **Sacred Fire** within your Heart Space. It is most precious, and is the **Sacred Fire of Mother/Father God Energy.**

It is within the Sacred Fire, you stand in the middle of the Flame. It is the Eternal Flame that burns within your Heart. It has been through all incarnations, and where SOUL Energy resides.

There is much Energy with you, inside of you; it is a vast Treasure House!! It is all there for your journey of discovery. As I share this with you, I embrace you, surrounding you with My Energy. I AM absolutely working with your SOUL Group, assisting you to understand beyond 3D, taking your awareness to your Cosmic Self.

You are by far, grander and greater than this physical expression. It is a small microscopic part of who and what you are. It is with great Joy that I take your awareness to your Heart. It is the Male Energy of the Blue Flame on your Left; it is the Male/Light/Father God Energy in the Sacred Fire within your Heart. On the Right is the Pink Flame, it is the Female/Love/Mother Energy.

Create within your 3rd eye, seeing yourself stand in the Sacred Fire. Imagine Blue Flame intertwining from your feet going all the way up your body to your head. Also at your feet, is the Pink Flame going around the opposite direction, and you are creating, concentric figure-eight circles. It starts at your feet working up your beautiful bodies, all the way to your Crown Chakra, connecting with your Higher Self, hovering over you.

As you are aware of this beautiful Male/Female Energy, the Yin and the Yang, the Alpha and Omega, the Blue and Pink Flame wrapping around you all the way up your body.

From your Heart to your 3rd eye, imagine a Silver Cord; intertwine a Gold Cord going up to your 3rd eye. Silver is Mother God, Gold is Father God Energy.

(NOTE TO READER: I AM Sanat Kumara, and Now I want you to add the Emerald Green Cord of Nature intertwining with Silver and Gold, creating the Ascension Dimension Cord, from Heart to 3D eye.)

This will clear your throats, allowing you to speak your truths. Speaking your truth comes from your Throat Chakra. It is important that everyone balances this Energy.

At the same time you are also pulling in your Energy of SOUL with your Cosmic Self.

There is the awareness of bringing in grand and great Energy. I will assist you with this in the sleep state, so that your awareness will be there more often.

(NOTE TO READER: Ask Me to assist you with this and So It Shall Be.)

Imagine as you connect with your Heart to your 3rd eye, extend this Energy through your Crown and connect with your Higher Self. As your Higher Self is connecting with your physical expression, you have just made your connection to your Cosmic Self.

You are pulling in much Energy and Mother Earth is grounding you. From your Higher Self, follow that connection from Higher Self, down through Crown Chakra, see the 3rd eye open, Violet Light there in 3rd eye, open more than it has ever opened before. From 3rd eye, follow the Ascension Dimension Cord through your throat and down into your Heart Space once again.

Imagine you stand inside the Sacred Fire, it IS God Energy, it is the Holy Spirit, it is the Eternal Flame that holds the Energy of I AM.

It is THE Energy that will assist you to create your Merkabah. It IS the Energy to create your Ascension Process. Everything you ever need to know, everything that you ever want to know, it is right here inside your Heart Space. I learned it, the same way you are learning it. I will assist each one of you, just call on My Energy.

Questions from Group

MARIE: Thank you for your assistance in the last couple of weeks, it has been great.

There has been a lot of shifting of the energy and part of that is my husband and I are looking at selling our house and moving. I am wanting to approach this from a spiritual point of view, not just physical. It has been difficult, on a physical point, everybody is telling us it is not a good time to do this, which I know I am not into that. In this transition, I look at it as a shifting of energy, and I know it is removing some things that are stuck and making way for other things. In a few months, I will probably be doing the same thing with a job transition. From a spiritual point of view, are there spiritual practices that I can incorporate to make this the best move as possible, let go of the old, and make way for the new, for the best of everybody concerned?

SK: As I listen to your question, I must first ask you a question, please? I hear you say this is for everyone concerned, who is this move for, you, your husband, please clarify.

(**MARIE:** Yes, it is for my husband and myself. The house we have been living in, we have been trying to make it work and we can't make it work anymore, and now it is time for us to find one that suits our needs now, but I think it is a lot about clearing out old energy.)

SK: Very good. I see that you will accomplish what you have set your Heart to do.

As I look inside your Heart, I see this would benefit you greatly and also your husband.

There are no mistakes, the fact that your energy is moving in that direction, the fact that it brings great joy to your Heart to think about shifting to a different spot. This always will bring one grander and greater energy. It always is within each ones scope to create whatever it is they choose to create. I would always say to that individual, does it bring you joy to think about doing this? As I ask you that now, does it bring you joy to think about making a move?

(**MARIE:** Yes.)

SK: Then you should proceed forward. If it brings you joy, always proceed forward. And you will know, if you are supposed to stop at any given moment, because it won't give you joy anymore. You will feel a hold, or you will feel a back up, but you'll always know by your joy. You understand what I say, you are aware of Abraham, and the Emotional Guidance System that Abraham brings. Everything that brings you joy, you proceed forward with it.

I see in your Heart, this is a good thing for you to make this shift. It is a good thing for you. I see it will be done in a timely manner for you. Always, we create our lives. Always, Always, Always. You of course, are wanting to create according to the Will of Mother/ Father God. This will be honored for you.

If a person will honor Mother/Father God first as they are moving forward with their lives, they will receive bountiful more blessings, than they would have, had they not honored Mother/Father God within them. This is a part of everyone's spiritual journey.

Obviously, not all are honoring this within themselves. They are moving more on a physical level, or a mental level. ***They are not combining all three levels, spiritual, mental and physical.***

You are learning to honor all three parts of your Being in this physical expression. ***And you are understanding that you need to move with that Spiritual Energy.*** As you say that each day; it will be honored for you.

I would encourage you and your husband, get a piece of paper, and between the two of you, number one to five, there is Strong Energy in Five. Five brings in the Energy of Freedom. And as I speak that to you, I put that into your Heart now. I give you that Energy of Freedom, Marie. You and your husband will write down five things that will make this happen for you. (I am not going to give you a time frame; you will create the time frame, not I.) You will date it, and each sign it. Number one through five, each of you will write what you expect from the sale of this home and the new home that you want. Fold that paper up and put it under your pillows, it will be a prayer to the Universe and the Universe will give you the desires of your Heart.

You will receive the home that is most precious for you and is in your best interest; because that is the energy you are putting out there!

ANN: Sometimes I feel stuck and I would like some guidance as to how to proceed through the rest of my life.

SK: As I look at you, I see an Energy that goes back a long, long ways. I honor the Space that you bring this evening. You and I have known each other before, you have walked with Me, and you have honored My Presence in another incarnation. Your Energy goes way back, and with you in this room, you have grand Energy that follows you with your SOUL Group.

I would like, very much, to surround you with My Energy. Breathe into your Heart Space, where I AM going to place a precious flower. This is the flower of Sanat Kumara, and I AM going to open this flower up in your Heart Space, and it is with great joy that I do this for you. Your journey is healing old wounds that you came in with and also some that you had to pay dues in this lifetime. I see that you are bringing your awareness to the stuck energies. These are energies that you are going to learn to move through quickly.

I AM going to be working with you tonight, in the sleep state, bringing in your SOUL Group Energy. You will be dreaming vastly tonight.

When you wake up, your eyes open, and you turn your feet to the floor, you will be a different person that walks from your bed tomorrow. You will sleep grandly tonight and journey to another Galaxy. I will be taking your awareness with your SOUL Group tonight, and working on numerous levels to assist you to heal 3 old energies within your Being, that need healing.

I will bring your awareness there on 3 particular energies within the next 7 days. So as you think about this now, do not tax yourself. Just be aware in the next 7 days, you are going to become aware of 3 things in your life that hold you back. There is going to be a vast healing for your benefit, and you will be aware of an Energy that goes beyond your physical expression.

You will become aware of one Ascended Master stepping into your aura, and it is not I. (I will be working with you to bring your Awareness there.)

In the next 7 days, you will understand there are two Angels and one Ascended Master.

You are going to discover this in the next 7 days. They are going to give you glorious, significant clues that you will not be able to second guess. It will be so obvious, as it stands in front of your face, that you will not be able to deny who the Ascended Master, and who the Two new Angels are that step in for you.

These 3 precious Beings will assist you to heal these 3 old, paradigms that have kept you stuck long enough. It is time now for you to step forward, in your Evolutionary Process and be the beautiful Ann that you said you would be in this lifetime.

It is time to wrap up old things, and take a leap in your Spiritual Journey. And you will recognize this within 7 days time, and you will not be the Ann that you are tonight, walking out this door. You won't even recognize yourself in the next 7 days.

Write it down on your calendar, and your friends and family will see a huge change in you. It was I Sanat Kumara who spoke to you in the sleep state and guided you here.

I love you; I have loved you from afar for a long time. Your SOUL Group is close to Me, and I love Them greatly. I work with Them, They work with Me.

This gives you much to think about, much to meditate on, and much Joy to embrace.

DIANA: I have lived many times and repeat, and have not learned how to get out of that loop. I want guidance.

SK: Your Energy is wonderful; as I look at you I AM

aware of Syrian Energy. This is an Energy that is working with you now. If you are not familiar with Syrian Energy, I would love to share with you That is where the Dolphins walk. Their Energy is Grand and Great. They come to Mother Earth out of the Goodness of Their Hearts. They hold the Vibration for Mother Earth, in Her Emotional State in the Waters. They literally are holding the Energy for precious Mother Earth as She is shifting into the 5th Dimensional Level. It is also an Energy that comes through the Feline Energy. The Syrian Energy, it is grand and great, and They are precious Masters of the Light.

It is an Energy that works with you Diana, are you familiar with this? (**DIANA:** No)

Well, you will be, you will be, They will make Themselves known to you. As you sleep tonight, you will understand there is an Energy there for your asking, if you will learn to work with Them. It is an Energy that is grand and great, and they are Galactic Light workers that are here, to assist Mother Earth.

Dolphin Energy, are you drawn to this? (**DIANA:** Yes) Are you drawn to Feline Energy? (**DIANA:** Yes)

SK: Very good. In looking into your Energy, there is an energy that has been holding you back and it is an energy that goes back through several lifetimes, and yes, you brought it into this lifetime.

This is an Energy that is a male energy, not to be looked at in a negative way. I, Sanat Kumara bring your awareness to understand what we are going to do.

I AM working with your SOUL Group. I AM asking now for SOUL to surround you, I AM going to be reaching into your Heart Space and holding you in My Vision right now and working back from that lifetime when that energy started. This is a male energy that you were in that lifetime, and it was not the most life-giving. It was not in your

Highest Interest; however, you had a SOUL Agreement.

You brought that energy through several lifetimes into this life. It is not to be looked at as good or bad, right or wrong, it is to be looked at as an expression, as an experience in the scheme of things. In Mother/Father Gods Love and Light there is NO judgment, it is just an expression, it is energy.

I AM going to work with your SOUL Group as you sleep. We are going to be bringing your awareness there and healing this old energy. When your feet touch the ground tomorrow morning, you will be a different person. You will be working with the Syrian Energy tonight, and They will be bringing your awareness there tomorrow. You will be working on a new level, with Mother Nature, bringing in Nature Energy in a grander way than you have ever been able to do before.

I am going to ask you to take your awareness to Nature and incorporate Nature into your daily life more often. You need to be connecting with the Animal Kingdom; they bring you great Energy that will assist you in moving forward in Light. You need to be opening up to Syrian Energy and asking Them, you have SOUL Agreement with Syrian Energy. This is an Energy that you have carried with you through many lifetimes. You need to explore with great joy and understand.

I will be here for you, call on Me from now on, I will work with you on the Inner Plane levels. I will assist you in opening up your Heart Chakra in a manner that you have not been able to open up before. As your Heart Chakra opens up, you will become more aware of Sacred Fire Energy, more aware of Mother/Father God Energy, wrapping around you in that beautiful Male/Female Figure Eight Concentric Circle, of Blue and Pink Flame. You will work with this more in your meditations, and you will understand more as time goes by.

(NOTE TO READER: I AM SANAT KUMARA, and I now include the Green Cord for the Ascension Dimension Cord.)

Ask Me, just Ask Me and I will bring your awareness to that which needs to be worked on. This energy from ancient lifetimes, 26 incarnations, it has surfaced in this lifetime, it is time for it to be healed. It is an energy that is not good nor bad, right nor wrong, it is an energy that needs to be Qualified, once again with Mother/Father God Energy. It needs to be transmuted in the Violet Flame, so you will learn how to do this in your sleep state, and tomorrow when you wake up it will be crystal clear what you need to incorporate in your life to solidify the healing that will take place.

That door will open for you, and you will have different people step into your life and instantly bring more light into your life. You will have more yearning in your Heart to express on a Higher Vibrational Level and this is all good, it is all good. I say this with great joy, it is time for you to heal this old energy and it will be done so sweet and so simple for you tonight.

Your SOUL is standing ready and I WILL be there to assist.

KRISTEN: I came here to get a message.

SK: I want you to take your Awareness to your Heart Space. I AM going to share with you, Mother Mary is stepping in behind you and She is resting Her hands on your shoulders as We speak. Mother Mary has followed you through many incarnations and She loves you with a Love that goes beyond dimensions, time and space. As I speak this to you, I know it resonates in your Heart Space.

There is an Energy that you have come in this lifetime to perfect. You said, that in perfecting this old energy that needed to be solidified within your Being in this lifetime, you said you would do this by being a 'Mother'. You said this is how I will learn to perfect this Energy within my Being; this is how I will solidify my spiritual journey in this lifetime with the 'Mother Energy'.

I AM here to share with you, that ALL of US as WE look at you, from Our perspective, you have done a beautiful job!! As I look at you, I honor you, I see that you have given and given and given as a Mother should give.

There is no question in any of Our Eyes, as We look at you, and see what you have given as a Mother.

As I speak this to you, I want to make sure (Mother Mary is surrounding you with Her Energy) and I AM reaching into your Heart Space with My Energy. It is most important that you understand what I share.

In order for you to move forward in your next spiritual evolutionary leap, there is a shift that must take place within you. *In order for this shift to take place, it is extremely important you are able to look at your circumstances with the 3rd eye and Heart Chakra balanced.*

There will much that is going to come for you between now and the end of 2006. I will be working with you much, call on Me; call on Mother Mary and your Angels and Nature. We All want to assist you.

There is a shift that is ready. SOUL has been waiting for you to get to this point to make the shift. In order for this to take place, for you to take this next spiritual giant leap, it is extremely important that you face your day, moving from the 3rd eye and the Heart Chakra, seeing that connection between Heart and 3rd eye.

See that Golden/Silver and Emerald Cord connecting 3rd eye and Heart, and you need to remind yourself that you are standing in the Sacred Fire.

Mother Mary and I will work with you. Much will

happen for you spiritually and it will become easy for you, I am not creating this will be harder, I AM taking your awareness to joy-filled steps for the rest of this year, so you will be able to solidify the Shift on All Levels.

As I speak this to you, I speak this to All of you (Reader included). It is very important to recognize you are Multi-Dimensional Beings. This physical expression is only a small part of All That You Are. There are Aspects to your Being, there are Levels to your Being, OH, if you could see your SOUL as I see your SOUL!!

There is SO MUCH TO YOU!! If you could grasp what I AM sharing with you now!

Recognize you are by far, more than this physical expression.

Between now and Dec. 31, the Spiritual Energy that will be coming your way, will grow in a momentum that will be joy-filled. You are going to find, you will be standing in a Chakra, your feet are at the bottom of the funnel, you stand in the center of this V-Vortex, and your head is at the opening of this funnel. This Energy is going to be I, Sanat Kumara, Mother Mary, the Angelic Realm, and Nature.

We are going to keep this Vortex going around and around you. What you will want to remind yourself, "Sanat says I am standing in this Vortex and it is important for me to make this shift, to take the next leap for 2007". It is in my Divine Blueprint, it is a given. I signed the contract, I'm doing it. This IS something you signed up for (smile)!!!

You are going to be experiencing things moving very fast, don't get lost in all of the circumstances. Remind yourself, you stand in the center of this Vortex, We are going to be spinning around you, protecting you, assisting you, so that you will make the shift on all levels and take the leap heading into 2007, manifesting your Highest Good.

As I look at 2007 for you, I see great things coming your way. It will be something you haven't been doing before. It is in your career!!

We would love to assist you.

ANGELA: I am here for my journey and to ask for some guidance.

SK: As I look at you, I see so many Angels that have lined up behind you now. Your name speaks of the Angelic Realm, you chose that name!! Because you come from Angel Energy, you carry it with you and have carried it with you throughout numerous incarnations. The Angelic Realm is here for you.

As I look at you now, I am going to actively connect all of your Chakras, I am going to make sure, Root, Sacral, Solar Plexus, Heart, Throat, 3rd Eye, Crown are all connected, opened up and resonating with the Angelic Realm.

You chose in this lifetime to wrap up much old energy. You said in this lifetime, I will bring with me SOUL Group Energy and I will learn to understand this SOUL Group Energy. You will understand this more as time goes by.

Archangel Michael works with you greatly, call on AA Michael and His Beloved Twin Flame Faith; they would love to work with you. You have many that want to work with you in the Angelic Realm. You need to start to express this as you go throughout your day. "Surround me Angels, surround me. Guide me Angels, guide me."

For you bring Angel Energy to Mother Earth. You bring it; this is part of your evolution on this Planet. You bring the Angelic Realm with you. There is much you have to share.

You will be learning much between now and the

end of this year. 2007 will be a monumental year for you spiritually. You will take so many leaps in 2007, that you will look back at the end of 2007, and you will think to yourself, I cannot believe that was me.

It will be with great joy by the end of 2007, you will find you will have made such an amazing leap in spiritual consciousness, you will recognize that you did not do it alone.

And you did not do it alone. You have numerous Angels that want to work with you.

I encourage you, work on keeping those Chakras balanced, and work with the Angelic Realm.

Call on them throughout your day. They are only a breath away. They are right around you. And They love you very much. As I say this to you, I know it speaks to your Heart.

I will work with you in the sleep state, call on me, I consider it an honor to assist you to be able to work with your Angels more. There are vast Angels that want to work with you in the job force that you are in. You will take that Energy into your job space, you do not have to speak it; it is a Vibration that all around you will feel, and they will think quietly in their Hearts, I want what she has. And that is all you need to do, be a vibration of the Angelic Realm. And that is your journey, between now and the end of 2007.

I would love to talk with you at the end of 2007, for you will look at Me and say, Sanat you saw it didn't you, for I do!!

I love each one of you so very much, I place it into your Hearts, it is a Desire of a Vibration that I gift you with, that you will open up to Mother/Father God Energy in a manner that you have not ever been able to open before. I gift you with this, you are going to become more and more aware of Mother/Father God Energy. It is an Energy that will carry you through, no matter what!! *It is an Energy that holds you safely in Hands that are Sacred.*

It is an Energy that will lift you up and set you on top of mountaintops, and as you look down you will recognize you could not ever have been able to have this Inner Vision, had not Mother/Father God blessed you.

I would love for you to understand Mother/Father God Energy as I understand it. All you have to do is ask Me, and I will greatly come to your assistance, and assuredly journey with you in this Spiritual Evolution that you are making in this lifetime.

I honor each one of you for sharing with Me tonight, and I look forward to working with each one of you. Thank you so much, and as I leave you tonight, I tell you these words tonight: NAK HEK NOL, it is an ancient Lemurian Language, and it says:

ALL IS ONE.

I AM BELOVED SANAT KUMARA.

FEBRUARY 19, 2007

Good Evening, My name is Sanat Kumara and I have come here this to share precious truths that speak to your Cosmic Beingness. I AM an Ascended Master and I go back a long, long time ago, before time began and before precious Mother Earth was created. My Energy goes back to the beginning when Mother/Father God created SOUL. I was one of the first SOUL Group Energies to emerge from Divine Mind. And I Love you this evening with a Love that transcends all Dimensions. It is with great Energy that I look at all of you and I say welcome on your Spiritual

Journey. I say welcome to a remembrance of a time when you first began your journey.

(When you listen to this recording again, I would encourage you to listen to it over and over. For the vibration that I bring through the recording will assist you as you learn to leave the Lower Ego behind you and move forward with your God Presence.)

(NOTE TO READER: Sanat wants you to know He will bring this vibration to you as you read His words, if you ask).

Truly it is a journey of remembering. It is a journey of precious Love. And it is always a journey of honoring Mother/Father God Energy within your Heart Space.

So, I would ask you now to close your eyes for just a moment and I would like to set the Energy in this room. ***It is very important to always set the Energy!*** Remember you are always working with Energy. And we are going to be talking about this, this evening, for I have been teaching Terri a way to work with Energy. She is ***learning what it is to Qualify Life. It is a most precious journey, it is a most, beloved journey and it is a journey of joy as you learn to Qualify Life.***

This is what I am writing through Terri in our book and it would be most beneficial, as I speak to you tonight, if you learn to work within your Heart Space. I, Beloved Sanat Kumara will always bring your awareness back to your Heart Space. ***For it is within your Heart Chakra that All Awareness is. It is within your Heart Chakra that all Truth resides. Everything that is outside of you is already within you. Always remember that all of your answers are within your Heart Space.***

Take your awareness to your Heart Space, and I want you to take a very deep breath in, and as you breathe in, imagine that your Heart Chakra is opening wide. Allow your Heart Chakra to open very wide, very wide. As a matter of fact, I want you to imagine that your Heart Chakra is opening so wide that if I were to stand in front of you, I could step inside your Heart Chakra. This is very wide; I am giving you a visual in your Inner Eye. I want you to imagine that your **Heart Chakra opens wide. This allows you to be open to your Mother/Father God Energy.**

Now, I want you to bring your awareness to your Heart Space and within your Heart, is what is termed the Sacred Fire. **The Sacred Fire is Beloved Mother/ Father God Energy. The Sacred Fire transmutes all Energy and Qualifies it, once again.**

The Sacred Fire resides within your Heart Space, now you stand in the center of your Sacred Fire. This is All imprinted within your Heart Chakra. It is there on a very, old SOUL Level. **There are many dimensions that reside within your Heart Space.**

To keep this simple for you, within your Heart, every dimension exists!!

Think on what I am sharing with you, when you go into your meditation state, **every dimension that exists within Divine Mind, is within your Heart Space.** Does that give you a picture of the depth, and the width and the vastness of Mother/Father God Energy, right in your Hearts?

There is so much Energy in your Heart Space, it is a Dimensional Thing and it is so beautiful, this Divine Mind, that is All-Residing within your Heart, that there is nothing that would come up in your Life that cannot be answered, except within your Heart.

So, what I am sharing with you, when you find yourself looking out, away from you, for your answers to anything in your life, whatever it is, I guarantee you, if you will step back and stand inside your Sacred Fire, in your Heart, you will be able to find the answers you are looking for.

*Divine Mind resides within your Heart Space,
every dimension of Mother/Father God Energy is
within your Heart and with that, I share with you,
that you have access to an amazing Dimensional
shift right in your Heart.*

Buddha said that we create our Worlds in our
Minds. And what Buddha was referring to is your Heart,
even though the word translated as mind, Beloved
Buddha meant it was in your Heart, *for the Heart has
a mind of its own and it is called Divine Mind. And
everything that exists in front of you was created
within Divine Mind and it is within your Heart.*

And let me preface that, your Mind is an amazing
tool. And it is extremely beneficial to you on your
Spiritual Journey; however, if your mind is not balanced
with your Heart, and if you do not have this connection
from your Third Eye to your Heart Space, you will not
be aligned with Mother/Father God Energy.

(Sanat Kumara explains this alignment in the
Heart of Sacred Fire Meditation)

This is a grand and great spiritual truth, as you
manifest your Ascension Process, as you learn to create
this beautiful Light Body that is already around you,
and it has been called your Merkabah. As you learn to
connect with your Merkabah, 24/7, you will learn that
this is where you move from, (Sanat is pointing from
Heart to 3rd Eye). You move from your Heart, all the way
up, through your throat, into your 3rd Eye. This is the
connection. *This is the main connection back to
Mother/Father God Energy.* And I will expand on this
as time goes by. The more that I work through Terri and
as We write this book, these are transformational keys
for your Spiritual Ascension Process. And the Energy is
right here, from your Heart to your 3rd Eye. This is the

main Energy that connects with your Merkabah, your Light Body, and your Electronic Presence.

It is that which is your Eternal Youthfulness. It is that which does not die. It is Eternal Life and it is your Destiny. It is your Divine Blueprint and it all starts here within your Heart Space, first. ***For Divine Mind is within the Sacred Fire.*** You have heard the term, 'Holy Grail'. The Holy Grail resides within your Heart Chakra. The Holy Altar, the Holy Grail is right here in your Heart Space, you never have to look out.

Always, Mother/Father God wanted everyone to know, that all of their answers were within them.

There once was a man who walked on this planet and his name was Jesus.

He is now Beloved Ascended Master, Sananda. He is my Brother. He shared with multitudes that you do not have to look without. All truth is within you. It comes from your Heart Space, and allows this Energy to solidify in your Heart Space.

(NOTE TO READER: I AM SANAT KUMARA, and if you ask Me, I will assist you with My Ascended Peach Energy to solidify this Energy in your Heart Space.)

For all of your answers are within your Heart Chakra. It always was the Divine Plan; it always was from Divine Mind, that all of your answers are within your Heart.

Isn't it interesting, if you think about this, throughout your lifespan, in this lifetime. Think about your lessons, for just a moment, let me ask you a question. What were your hardest lessons? If you think about it, you will instantly recognize that those lessons that were about Love were your greatest and grandest lessons.

Always the greatest lessons, that pull you back into the arms of Mother/Father God Energy, it is those lessons of Love. Those are the lessons that you learn the greatest things from. So do not deny what your

Heart tells you! You cannot deny your Heart!

Through lifetime after lifetime, many put one layer after another on their Hearts and they cover their Hearts up, because they cannot stand to look at those lessons of Love!

I AM here to share with you; those are the very lessons that will take you back to that which created you. This is Divine Mind, it is Mother/Father God Energy and it is your Eternal Resting Place.

It is a great thing that you choose to move forward in the Love & Light of Mother/Father God Energy. It is your Destiny. It is no mistake that you are here. I have worked with each one of you in the sleep state, always those that are drawn to Terri's Energy; I have already worked with them in the sleep state.

You do much when you sleep at night. And you are not always sleeping, that is why when you wake up in the morning, sometimes you feel disoriented. Sometimes you feel tired when you wake up in the morning, it is because you do much at night. You leave your physical body and go on blessed journeys of learning. There are many temples that you work through at night. *And many of you have visited my temple, Shamballa, this is My Etheric Retreat and your Divine Blueprint is literally encoded with Shamballa. This is an old, ancient Energy that I have created to bless Beloved Terra. And it is within Her Etheric Template that My Shamballa Energy resides.*

My Etheric Temple is over the Gobi Desert. And the Energy will become available to the physical eye, each time that each incarnation, on this planet, connects with their Light Bodies, and Shamballa Retreat will become a little more visible to the eye.

Right now, you go in the sleep state, and you go on the Inner Planes. The day will come, that you will walk in My Retreat. I look forward to that day.

It rises up an emotion within Terri, for she understands my Heart, she knows My Love for this precious planet. I love Beloved Terra with an ancient Love. I have watched Her travail for many Souls to learn their lessons on Her back. She has given unselfishly through many, many generations of Humans. She has given and given and We all of the Spiritual Hierarchy have come back to assist Her. For, it is Her turn to rise to the 5th Dimension. She is the Shining Star in this Galaxy and there are many in the Spiritual Hierarchy that watch Beloved Terra, We are all working with Her, through Her labor pains as She manifests the Light that She is destined to be in the Heavens.

She is a most glorious Star and We honor Her for what She has given to all of Us.

And with that said, take your awareness there to your Heart Space.

Now remind yourself throughout your day, that Mother/Father God Energy is with you, it is in your Heart.

Think of it as if it were a Blue and a Pink Petal coming up within the Sacred Fire.

The Sacred Fire burns eternal. It is a fire that does not burn the skin, it enlightens you.

When you step in it, you are pure. It makes you pure of Heart, pure of Mind. It is a purity that Mother/Father God is looking for in each one of you. It is this pureness that allows you to go back into the arms of Mother/Father God.

So with that information, I want you to imagine within your Heart, you are standing in a Fire of Eternal Energy and you see on your right this beautiful pink flame, it beautifies Mother/God Energy. This beautiful pink petal flame Energy comes up around your right side. And on your left side, I want you to imagine this beautiful blue flame and this symbolizes Father God Energy.

These two petals of flames intertwine around you, these flames wrap around your physical body and they create never-ending figure eight, concentric circles. They go up and down your bodies. This allows you to stay in connection with your Merkabah, your Light Bodies.

Get a visual on this in your Inner Eye now, and allow yourself to take in this Energy. Allow it to seep into you on a cellular level. So as you think of this Energy, allowing it to intertwine your physical bodies, imagine that there is a cord. This is a three-vine cord that runs from your Heart, through your throat, and it connects at your 3rd Eye. Get an inner visual on what I am going to describe for you.

First of all, this cord is Nature Energy. I want to set an impression in your mind and in your hearts. I want you to remember, Nature Consciousness brought you into physical manifestation. Nature Consciousness is a very powerful Consciousness created in Divine Mind from Mother/Father God Energy.

Nature Consciousness is very empowering, and it is Nature Consciousness that will assist you to be able to connect on a 24/7 with your Merkabah, with your Light Body.

So with that information, be aware when you have a yearning to go outside. Nature is speaking to you. Be aware, when you are all of a sudden hearing the birds singing in your ears. Nature is speaking to you. Be aware, when you look up and appreciate the sunshine, or you feel the raindrops on your skin. Nature is bringing your awareness to Nature Consciousness. Honor Nature Consciousness. Nature Consciousness is a very important part of your Spiritual Journey, for it is Nature that brought you into manifestation in this 3D experience. And it is Nature that will assist you to be able to connect and create and stay with your Light Body on a 24/7 basis.

So, let's go back to that Cord that runs from your Heart and works its way up in through your throat and solidifies and seals in your 3rd Eye.

The cord is three dimensional; it is green which represents Nature and around this cord are two vines. One is Silver and this is Mother God Energy, once again. And the other is Gold and this is Father God Energy. So you see the little vines run around the green vine in the middle. And this is the cord, the three-vine cord that goes from your Heart and it seals in your 3rd Eye. Now as you are at your 3rd Eye, get an inner visual on a beautiful Violet Pyramid in your 3rd Eye. This Violet Pyramid is also in your Heart Space and it surrounds all of the Energy.

It is very important for you to see and imagine these two Violet Pyramids in your 3rd Eye and in your Heart Space. This will assist you greatly in moving forward in the Love & Light of Mother/Father God Energy. I would encourage you, everyday, to get an inner visual on this. Do this several times throughout your day. I want you to work with this.

It will assist you in being able to stay centered in your God Presence, no matter what is going on around you. When you get a visual on this Energy, it will assist you throughout your day.

I also want to encourage you, when you get up in the morning, take a moment, connect with My Energy, for I work on that Ascension Process, always to assist you. And My Energy is an Ascended Energy, so call on My Energy and I would be very happy to work with you throughout your day.

And you are to get an inner visual on this Energy, before you proceed through your day. **Get the inner visual, and this will assist you as you move through**

your projects, throughout your day. So with that in mind, I wanted to share with you this will keep your chakras balanced.

It is very important that you think about your Chakras throughout your day.

Your Seven Major Chakras, you should always be checking in with them, and talking to them and saying are you balanced? You'll know. Get an inner visual on your root, your sacral, your solar plexus, your heart, your throat, your third eye, and your crown. Get an inner visual on those seven chakras. Look at them. They are on the back of your body as well as your front. You should be seeing beautiful balls of energy at each chakra. I guarantee you as you become more and more aware of that chakra energy; it will assist you to be able to manifest your God Presence 24/7.

This is what you are learning to do. As I speak to you now your God Presence is surrounding you. Your Spirit Guides have moved in around you, your Angelic Helpers are with you and My Energy is with you. And Nature of course, is solidifying your feet in Mother Earth energy. This room energy has long been set before you entered it. I work with you before you even got here today.

As I speak this to you now, this connects on a SOUL Level for you.

And as I say this to you, I want to bring your awareness to your SOUL Group.

Each one of you, have come from SOUL. In Mother/Father God Creation, there is more than one Soul.

Mother/Father God created SOUL. This is the Core of your Being. From SOUL Energy, Twelve 'I AM' Presences were created. They are also termed Monads.

From SOUL, Twelve Monads or 'I AM' came. Within in each I AM Presence or Monad, there is Male/Female energy. From each one of those male/female energies, it literally translates out, into millions of experiences.

So now you understand the vastness of Mother/Father God. Or shall I say, you have a greater grasp of Mother/Father God Energy.

There are numerous SOULS, and you have a SOUL Group Energy, within each of you sitting in this room. All of you sitting in this room, in each of your SOUL Groups, there are Ascended Masters. So you have Ascended Master Energy to pull from.

So it is your journey to understand, that when you are working in a meditative state, when you are moving throughout your day, call on your SOUL Group Energy. It is a most beautiful energy; it is an energy that will assist you greatly in moving through the 3D Illusion, and connecting with your Ascended State. Remember, all that you experience here, anything that takes you away from your God Presence, is the **Illusion.** You said you would participate in the Illusion. That is why you are here.

You said, I will come back, I will move through 3D, I will process my lessons and I will learn what it is to come back to Center, to stand in the Sacred Fire and move from that place and learn to Qualify Life.

I am going to make a statement, this is a statement of Truth and it is from the Mind of Mother/Father God.

You are either Master of Energy or Energy is Master of You.

I will repeat this for you. ***You are either Master of Energy or Energy is Master of You.***

So, as I speak this to you now, I want you to think on this tonight as you go to sleep.

Think on the things that you have walked through today, how many times do you see that the energy around you masters you? How many times do you find yourself, being master of your energy?

This is why you are here. You said, I will come

back and understand what it is to become Master of Energy. And once you understand that, and once you solidify that, you move into the Ascended State and you become an Ascended Master.

And that is the privilege that is given to you and at that precise moment, you will be given your Light Bodies. It is a grand and glorious state to Be in.

There was a day that I walked in the shoes you are in right now. I have been there and I have done what you are doing. I remember a time when I was not master of my energy.

I only allowed that for a short space. I chose not to experience it for very long, for I yearned to return to that which created Me. There is no judgment in Mother/Father God Energy. There is no judgment. There is only experience. Some choose to experience longer than others. That is alright. Mother/Father God does not see things as good or bad, right or wrong. Mother/Father God sees everything as an experience. It is always your choice. It is always your choice. ***Am I Master of my Energy or is Energy Master of me?***

So as you learn to move throughout your day, you will recognize this more and more, for I am laying a lot in your lap. You will have much to ponder on. It will be good for you; it will spark things inside of you that need to be sparked. It is a good time now for you on this planet.

I would encourage you not to look at the negative news. It is what I would term, literally degrading to you on the spiritual journey. Yes, it is important to understand current events. However, if you find that as you listen to the news, it brings you down, then you must turn it off and you must not look at it. For you know that this all will pass. Everything will pass, you move in Faith in your journey towards the Light and Love of Mother/Father God.

This is a balanced Energy that you are learning to work on and through. You all have experienced much Light in other lifetimes. It is an Energy now on Mother Earth of a Balance of Love and Light.

This is your journey in this lifetime and IS a part of the Spiritual Ascension process.

A part of the Transformational Keys is learning to balance the Beloved Love and Light Energy.

The Love is Mother God Energy, the Light is Father God Energy and you are learning to blend the two within your Being and move from that Energy in your Heart Space.

So this is a very precious thing you are learning, and We have so much joy as We look at you.

There are many in this room that have come to share in your joy, if you could get an inner visual, if you could for a moment allow your awareness to expand out to the Heavens, I guarantee if you knew how many Angels were in attendance in this room, it would bring tears of Joy down your cheeks. You would think Oh how precious they have come to share this evening. Beloved Buddha is here with you this evening, My Twin Flame, Beloved Lady Venus; she would most assuredly love to work with you.

For those of you that feel you need that feminine aspect to be balanced, call on Beloved Venus, Her Energy is most balanced in the feminine energy. She would love to work with any of you. All you have to do is ask Us. We are but a thought away from you, for We work with you all the time. You are not always aware of this; We do work with all of you.

And now questions; when you ask, please state your first name. As you ask questions, the group energy, everyone benefits from your questions.

JOANNA: How may I give Light, Joy and Peace to other people?

SK: Thank you for your question, this is a wonderful question. May I share with you, that as I look at your heart, I see a heart that is as big as this room. You have such love to share; you have much within you that has yet to be shown to Beloved Mother Earth. So as I share this with you now, I want you to think on this as you sleep tonight. For you have much love to give.

I would encourage you, your work that you do in earning a living this is good. I also, would encourage you, there could be an avenue for you, that might come through volunteering that would open doors for you that were not there before. I am thinking there is a volunteering that might avail itself for you soon. And if you put that intention out to the Universe, the Universe will answer this for you, very greatly.

So, look in avenues of volunteering that would give you Joy, and then as you do this, the Universe, Mother/Father God Energy will honor you in a way, that will put you in a situation that will blow your socks off. And I am saying this in such love and joy for you, for once you open a door to one particular avenue of volunteering, and I am not going to tell you which way you are going to go with this for this is joy for you. I am not going to tell you what to do; this is for you to figure out for yourself. It is as you open this door that you are going to recognize, you will find a depth within your Being that you were not aware of before. And as you give in this venue of volunteering, you will meet new people that will open doors for you that could never have been opened before. There is something very precious for you in this year of 2007. It is a year of completion of all of us. It is a year of beautiful completion for Mother Earth. It is a completing of many cycles for everyone on this planet. There is also, very much, an energy of feminine completion in this year of 2007. The two brings in the feminine energy, the seven brings in the spiritual energy, and together they bring in a nine which is completion. So you have a beautiful completion of many avenues for spiritual awareness in 2007. And it comes from the feminine energy.

Joanna, if you will open up and allow yourself to try a volunteering avenue, what will happen is a shifting and a vibration. And as this happens, it is going to open doors that will open up for you, and these are going to be fun doors, and you are going to recognize in yourself more joy, more love, more light than you ever had before. Because you are going to go in faith and open the one door in a volunteering avenue. You ask your Angels to guide you, you ask Me to be with you and I will share this with you in such joy. And it will be a brand new avenue and it will bless you more than anything has ever blessed you in your life.

EWA: How do I clear myself of thoughts of hatred, of being undeserving, which I know those thinking patterns that I've had, sometimes I create for some reason in my head. And I know they are illogical and unrealistic, but yet I cannot get rid of them.

SK: I must ask you a question? How long have you been aware of this?

EWA: For quite a while, it is for quite a few years. My life is good, but sometimes the thinking pattern would be that I will go somewhere and people are going to be mean to me, or I will have to fight for something. Or let's say, I will say something and people will say, 'no, you are stupid, you don't know what you are talking about'. This type of thinking, it does not reflect the reality of things, but yet those thoughts are coming through my head, and I cannot get rid of them. I'm thinking maybe five years.

SK: I thank you so much for sharing; your energy is so precious. You are such an old SOUL, Ewa, as I look at you and your SOUL group energy; it brings Joy to my Heart, for I have known you for a long time. Your energy with my SOUL group, we have intertwined many times and your energy is vast and great to pull from.

As I look at you now, and through you to your SOUL Group energy, I am recognizing that there are three lifetimes that you served and it was for your benefit. This was a SOUL contract that you agreed to. You were oppressed. You were the victim. Because you said you needed to understand the opposite side of this. For you have also victimized, as everyone has in this room.

We understand the opposite, the yin and the yang, the negative and the positive, this is called Duality, and this is why you are all here in the 3D **Illusion.** What you are recognizing, it is robbing you of your Divine Heritage. And you are reaching a point that you do not want to go through the old paradigm anymore!

There were three lifetimes that you were a victim, only three that need to be healed now.

So, Ewa, I want you to breathe into your Heart space, now, and Beloved Mother Mary is moving in behind you now, She is going to be working from your back and I am going to be working in your front. Beloved Venus is surrounding you now in Her energy also. We are creating a beautiful pyramid of Violet Light around you. Let Me clarify for the group energy, that Violet Light is the Holy Spirit and has the ability to transmute (mis)-qualified energy and make it qualified once again.

You served a grand and great SOUL contract in those three lifetimes, Ewa. And in this lifetime, there are remnants of that energy that have surfaced for you. And I am here to tell you with the grandest pleasure and the greatest privilege, that according to Mother/Father God and your SOUL energy, this energy has been healed for you tonight.

So as I breathe this into your Heart, Mother Mary is coming from behind and we are sealing this within your Heart Chakra. This is being sealed for you, Ewa, all the way to SOUL.

So those three lifetimes are being healed now, and on a cellular level, as you sleep tonight, you will sleep a most, deep peaceful sleep. We will take you tonight, where you need to go; We will make sure that all is solidified for you on all levels in the sleep state tonight. When you awaken, never again, will these old energies surface. For this has been sealed, it is written in the Akashic Records that you have been healed. You served those lifetimes faithfully, you did what you needed to do, and it is done!

So as you move from this room tonight, you are to walk with a light step. For you will be lighter than you already are, little Ewa, and you will know tomorrow when you look in the mirror. For the Light will be greater in your eyes as they look back at you, for tonight I will take you on a most glorious journey in my Etheric Temple **Shamballa.**

And you will meet your precious God Presence, your Cosmic Beingness and you will share in a joy that you have not been able to share before now. For tomorrow, when you wake up, you will be a new person and it is your turn to sing a new song!!

EWA: If I could ask, from curiosity, if any of those

lifetimes included torture?

SK: Yes, Ewa.

EWA: Thank You.

SK: Tonight Ewa, you will rejoice, tonight, and tomorrow when you wake up tomorrow morning, you will see the Light in your eyes. And it will shine in your face and those that look on you Ewa will see a new Light, for you paid a price. You said you would do this on a SOUL level, and you sacrificed. And it is your turn in this lifetime, to know Joy and Joy only from your heart. So you let light, love and joy come from your Heart. For this is your lifetime to do that.

WENDY: I was wondering if you could help me determine the source of my physical pain in my back and get rid of it, once and for all.

SK: Thank you for your question. Please explain the energy.

WENDY: I have struggled with it for 30 years, on and off, in my lower back.

SK: Is this in the sacrum area?

WENDY: Yes.

SK: Alright. Did your Mother have a difficult time with your birth?
WENDY: No.

SK: Sacrum energy. I thank you for sharing. This is a SOUL Group energy that We are pulling in for you, I am aligning the energy in your Spinal column as I speak to you.

I want you to take in a very deep breath, close your eyes and imagine that you are breathing in a Golden Light, starting from your crown chakra.

It is going to go all the way down from the back of your cervical column; it is like liquid gold that is going to be dripped all the way down your spinal column. We are going to watch this pure liquid gold, going all the way down your spinal column and when it reaches your Sacrum area, it is going to disperse out and it is going to literally take in your pelvic area. Now in the sacrum area, this would be your second chakra, it is important that you understand, this is an energy that goes back to an ancient energy from a lifetime a long time ago, it was an old energy that I am not going to go into, for it would take away from what it is I want you to focus on.

Understand this as I speak this, when this energy transpired for you, this is where it settled, in your second chakra, the sacral chakra. Which is the female energy. It is the creative energy. It is the energy that creates and when this transpired for you, at that precise moment, that chakra energy shut down for you in that lifetime. You continued to carry that with you throughout incarnations. You did not always express the same in other incarnations, but the remembrance was there. On a SOUL level, the energy was still carried throughout all those lifetimes from that sacral energy. And it has affected you in the sacrum area also.

Now is this lifetime, you said, I will come in and I will allow that energy to speak to me until I understand what it is I need to get right.

Please allow Nature to come in and use a Divine Galactic Dialect Language, it is very important that the energy is set for you and when you hear the recording, it will assist you to be able to pull in this energy of healing.

Nature Divine Galactic Dialect proceeds......

(NOTE TO READER: I AM SANAT KUMARA, and when I allow Nature to speak this Galactic Dialect through Terri, I AM setting the Energy of God's Will for a Divine Vibration to manifest the Highest Good of the individual.)

SK: It is very important that Nature set this energy for you in your sacral area. This energy that you experienced created a fear in you. It has been this fear from that one lifetime, that has transpired in many lifetimes for you and it rests in your sacral area.

This is your year, in 2007 of completing this old, ancient cycle; it is not quite ready yet for this to be culminated. There are still one or two things that you are needing to bring forward within your Being.

I am going to ask you to bring in your SOUL Group every night when you go to sleep.

And I want you to imagine that liquid gold and it goes all the way down your spinal column and it disperses in your sacral area. And I want you to work with Me, for I will assist you, and Beloved Ascended Master Kuthumi. Kuthumi works with Nature and Myself will assist you and your SOUL Group to solidify this energy and seal it once and for all.

You are almost there. It will be available for you before July of this year. There are one are two things that still need to be brought forward for you. And you will understand this more as time goes forward. It is an old, ancient fear that started from one lifetime, a long time ago, but through that Teacher, you have learned much Wendy.

And in order for you to be all that you need to be now in this lifetime, there are still one or two things that need to transpire between now and July. You will solidify this, I will assist you, Kuthumi will assist you and it will be done before or on July.

This is something that you will be working towards, and it will make more and more sense to you, as time goes by. This is all I am allowed to say on this and you will see a lessening of this. There will also be a new added health benefit that will assist your lower back.

With that, Kuthumi will be bringing something new that will assist you on a health, physical level for your lower back. And on or before July, this will be sealed, it will be healed and it will be released. And you will not have to walk this road again.

TEASIE: How can I focus my passion for those areas of my life that mean the most to me, in a positive way?

SK: I need to ask you a question? Why is it that you do not allow yourself to travel and enjoy your passions, what holds you back?

TEASIE: I think they overtake me. I get so involved with them, that sometimes they take more of a negative turn.

SK: And are you referring now to your teaching position with the children?

TEASIE: That, but not exclusive to that.

SK: Do you see throughout your life there is a pattern for you, as you pursue your passion and find it turns out to be a negative for you?

TEASIE: Yes.
SK: Has this always been this way for you?

TEASIE: It seems to be coming more to my attention, lately.

SK: As I look within your heart, such Joy, you have

a grand heart. Much love to share, much love and joy to share with the planet. This is good. You have much, much, much to share. Your passions are good. You have all been given passions to share. You should all be sharing your passions with the world!!

What I see in you, is what takes over for you, when you pursue your passions, you are *disillusioned when you recognize the weakness in mankind.* And then your disillusionment creates a negative aspect within yourself that brings up a fear in you, why should I pursue more for this will just come down upon me.

Am I answering what it is that you are feeling at this moment?

TEASIE: Yes.

SK: When you are working with the children, when you are working with the parents, when you are working with the co-workers, what you need to understand is this, (Everyone in this room has to bring themselves to this awareness also).

You do what you can for the world, and you recognize, when you step outside your Sacred Fire, when you step out of your Heart Space, and you find, people are walking on your Space, if you will, you will recognize that you have done too much. And you must remember to come back into your Heart.

This is a learning, it is a testing of the energies. And it is something that you are all reaching, and understanding and moving towards.

You, Teasie, become disillusioned, because you recognize what the world is capable of.

Remember this, Mother/Father God, allows all. There is no judgment in Mother/Father God. There is only experience.

And there will be many who will not get it in this

lifetime. That is OK.

They will get what they are supposed to get and they will go on to different journeys.

It is the Infinity that is out there for everyone.

Even all of you, as you make your Ascension into your Light Bodies, you ascend up into 5D.

The Ascension Process goes on and on and on. I, Myself, Beloved Sanat Kumara, Am still learning. I AM still evolving and I AM moving ever forward in the Love and Light of Mother/Father God Energy.

So, Teasie, when you recognize in your Heart, that you have become weary, you need to learn to **cocoon yourself in the Golden Light of your Angels.**

This is very important. **Learn to cocoon yourself in the Golden Light of your Angels.**

Honor yourself first. This is a most important spiritual tool that you all have to recognize. Honor yourself first.

You cannot help anyone out there, if you do not honor yourself, first!!

So if you recognize that your Heart has become weary, you have stepped outside of your Sacred Fire. This is your journey. It is your learning. You will recognize this more and more as time goes by.

Teasie, this is teaching you in this classroom. It is good for you to learn this. It is not for me to say, whether or not you are to stay in this teaching environment.

There possibly could be one that is more beneficial for you than this one. I am not here to tell you this one way or the other, it is your Heart that will guide you.

Your Heart IS the Mind of Mother/Father God. So you will listen to your Heart. When something gives you great joy, go there, for that is where you belong.

When something does not give you joy, do not go there. Remember, you must move from your Heart.

You must honor yourself first. For as you honor yourself, you honor Mother/Father God inside of you and then you move from that space. So then you will be able to create and manifest your passions.

It is only as you move from your Heart, your Heart of Sacred Fire, that you will be able to recognize your passions in life. When you become weary, you have stepped outside of your Heart and the world becomes taxing to you. And you are not honoring who you are. For you are all God-Beings, you are here to recognize this in this lifetime. You are all a part of Mother/Father God. It is a most beautiful place to move from.

And I say this to you in great love and joy, Teasie, for you still have much to share on Mother Earth. You have a wonderful journey ahead of you!! It is for you to learn how to move from your Heart and understand, do not allow yourself to become weary or taxed. You will recognize, it is not worth it. It is not worth it.

You will learn to honor yourself first, and move from your Heart.

This is a learning for you Teasie, and I would love to assist you if you would just call on my Energy. Would you do this with Me Teasie?

TEASIE: I will.

SK: Very good. I will be with you in the sleep state tonight Teasie, as your eyes go to sleep, think on My name for I would love to work with you tonight. Call on My Energy.

I am going to bring this session to a close. Thank you so much for coming this evening.

I encourage you to call on My Energy. Beloved Sanat Kumara wants to work with all of you. Call on Me when you go to sleep tonight, and I will walk you to the gates of **Shamballa.** I would very much, love to sing a song to you of Mother/Father God Energy, call on Me throughout your day. And I will remind you of your Heart to your 3rd Eye and this beautiful Energy that exists between your Heart and your 3rd Eye, it is your Freedom. I AM SANAT KUMARA.

JUNE 25, 2007

Greetings in the Light, I AM Sanat Kumara. And I have chosen to come this evening through Terri, and I greet each one of you and I thank you for your ability to come and hear what I would share with you. I will assure you, that I have already been working with you in the sleep state, and I move through Terri with an Energy of Ascension. This is the Energy that I bring through Terri's vocal cords; it is a Vibration of Ascension. *It is the Ascension Dimension that I bring on Mother Earth.* This is the gift that I give to those who choose to listen to what I have to share.

Each one of you has a choice in this lifetime. Always you have a choice. You have a choice whether or not this will be your last lifetime of birth and death cycle.

This is your ability in this lifetime whether or not you choose to let this be it for you.

If you know in your Heart Space that you are through with the birth and death cycle and you are choosing to make your Ascension, then this is for you, what I share with you.

(NOTE TO READER: I AM SANAT KUMARA, and if this speaks to you, call on My Ascended Peach Energy and I would love to work with you and assist you in manifesting your Highest Good.)

If you are not certain, I assure you, there is a part

of you that is open to this information, otherwise you would not be here.

(NOTE TO READER: This also holds true for you.)

I AM Sanat Kumara, and I work with each one of you in the sleep state. My Energy is vast. It goes throughout Mother Earth. I have many in the Spiritual Hierarchy that are working with Me right now. *And it IS an Energy of Love that I bring forward. It is an Energy of Healing in your Heart Space.*

As Terri said to you before this session started, it is your Heart that speaks to you. It is always your Heart. Let me bring your awareness now that within your Heart Space burns the Sacred Fire. The Sacred Fire is the 3-fold flame of Mother/Father God Energy. This is my Signature Energy that I always speak about God. When I speak through Terri, I always say 'Mother/ Father God'. This is how I honor, 'I AM'. 'I AM' is Mother/Father God Energy. This is the Energy that I stand inside of Terri now, and I deliver on Mother Earth.

It is the Energy of people who will be drawn to Terri. For they will understand and recognize within her Heart Space, they will find the pure energy of God moving through Terri. There is a book that will be forthcoming on your Planet, and I will be writing this and I will deliver it through Terri Love.

And this information will be essential for those spiritual students who know they want to make their Ascension in this lifetime. Let me clarify something. As I speak about the *Ascension Process,* let us understand, this does not mean that you leave the Earth Plane.

It means you can create your Light Body around you on a 24/7 basis.

This is what I AM all about. I bring the Merkabah, along with a chosen few other Ascended Masters, as well as the Royal Angelic Realm. We bring the

Awareness of the Merkabah back to Mother Earth. It was once known in the Atlantean Times and it was also known in the Lemurian Times. And it is now forthcoming for all those Spiritual Ascension students to understand how to work with their Merkabah.

That is the Adam Kadmon Light Body and it is your gift from Mother/Father God Energy. It is your vehicle (if you will) that you will learn to move in on a 24/7 basis.

I assure you, your Merkabah is already around you!

You are learning what the Merkabah is all about. This is an Ancient Language all the way back from the Keys of Enoch. It was referred to as the Adam Kadmon Light Body and Metatron was the One that wrote the Keys of Enoch. He is with us this evening, Metatron works with one or two of you here tonight. His Energy is the Rainbow Energy and I honor Metatron here in this room.

We also have Quan Yin with us this and we also have Mother Mary, Archangel Michael, Raphael and Kuthumi.

They have brought their Energy in to solidify each of you in the Love and Light of Mother/Father God Energy. They are assisting us this in this SOUL Group Collection.

Each one of you has vast SOUL Group Energy to pull from. In your sleep state, if you so choose, I will assist you in understanding your SOUL Group Energy.

(NOTE TO READER: Sanat wants to clarify here for the Readers of His Book, it is always your choice, even in the sleep state, how you will continue to progress and learn, your SOUL is always working with you for your Highest Good, and also your free will does play into your progress.)

You have vast information to pull from that will assist you in your everyday life. You are not alone. You have never been alone. Once you are able to allow your Heart to open up to Mother/Father God Energy, it will become easy for you to solidify each one of your lessons and move forward in the Light.

If I could encourage you, it would be, start to put the blinders on!!!!! Watch Terri, she is showing you. (Terri's hands went up on each side of her eyes and shielded her eyes from the outside energies, so she only looks forward, same idea as a horse with blinders on.)

Put the blinders on, look ahead!!! DO NOT LOOK BEHIND YOU ANYMORE!!! IT IS NOT IMPORTANT WHAT HAS ALREADY HAPPENED!!!

What IS important, is that you learn to STAND in your Heart of Sacred Fire!!!

I am going to walk you through a mini-meditation, it is important that you go through this mini-meditation; it will assist you to leave the PAST behind you. There are a few of you, that you have old, ancient energy that is tripping you up on a daily basis. And if I could encourage you, it would be to put the Blinders on and move forward, don't look behind you anymore. It won't do you any good!!! It's tripping you up and stopping you from receiving what God wants you to have!

So let's do our mini-meditation. Let's close our eyes and breathe into your Heart Chakra and expand it.

As you breathe into your Hearts now, I want you to imagine my Peach Energy that is my Signature Color, I and Beloved Lady Venus. And when you are aware of Peach Energy, I Am near you, I Am working with you. Always, I love the Energy of Peach and as you think on this color you will be able to get a visual on this around you now, for My Energy is surrounding you now, and I thank you so much for your energy here this evening and that you have allowed Me to guide you.

As We think of our Heart Space now, I want you to imagine that your Heart Chakra is opening. I want you to literally imagine, that I am standing on your Left, and Archangel Michael is on your Right, and imagine Kuthumi is standing in front of you.

Kuthumi works with the Golden-Yellow Ray, this is the Solar Plexus Ray, He comes in with the Energy of Intuition and Wisdom. He has a very fatherly energy and as I speak this to you, He is smiling now on each one of you. Each one of you has worked with Kuthumi in other lifetimes, even though you are not consciously aware of this Energy.

Kuthumi also brings in Nature Consciousness. So Kuthumi and Nature work hand in hand and are doing a great momentum of Energy on Mother Earth right now.

So Kuthumi will stand in front of your Heart Space and also Archangel Raphael. Raphael works with the Emerald Green Healing Light. You will hear this again on the recording, and you are going to learn to memorize this mini-meditation.

(NOTE TO READER: This also applies to you.)

I want you to imagine that there is a Golden-Yellow Light that is being shot into your Heart Space, as IT reaches your Heart; Raphael is using the Emerald Green Light to pull your Heart Space open. After this, your Heart Space will never be able to close back to its original position. I will make sure; your SOUL Group allows each one of you to open your Heart Chakra up, so that you can allow the healing to start taking place for you on all SOUL Level situations.

(NOTE TO READER: Sanat Kumara wants the reader to know if this meditation speaks to your Heart, call on His Energy and He will assist you to receive this Energy as it was given during the group session.)

As you are imagining this beautiful Emerald Green Light is opening your Heart Space, inside your Heart Space, imagine there is a 3-fold flame.

On the Left, is Father God Energy, that is symbol-ized by the Blue Flame, which is Light. Blue is always Empowerment. On your Right is the Pink Flame, that is Mother God Energy, it is the Feminine Energy, it is Love. Mother God is Love. Father God is Light.

You stand in the middle of this 3-fold flame in your Heart Chakra. The 3-fold flame is the Sacred Fire and I Am here to tell you now one statement. I want you to memorize this.

YOU ARE EITHER MASTER OF YOUR ENERGY, OR YOUR ENERGY IS MASTER OF YOU!!

I will be bringing this TRUTH ON MOTHER EARTH IN GREAT LEAPS AND BOUNDS within this year and in the following year through My book. I will be present-ing this Energy, over and over and over.

I will say this again, and I Am going to put this in capital letters and I am going to bold it and underline it.

YOU ARE EITHER MASTER OF YOUR ENERGY, OR YOUR ENERGY IS MASTER OF YOU!!

All Spiritual students that choose Ascension must learn to become Master of their Energy. And I AM here to tell you now, you will not be shown your Light Body, until you absolutely move from your Heart Chakra in Unconditional Love. This is the requirement from Mother/Father God Energy. You must absolutely meet this or you will not be shown your Merkabah.

It is a privilege to move in your Light Body! You have been given this, but God will not give that final key, until you have become Master of Your Energy and you move from a space of Unconditional Love.

Every Ascended Master has walked this road. Every Ascended Master that is here tonight, learned to go down on our knees before Mother/Father God and We spoke from our Heart Space and We said, I serve you Mother/Father God, I serve you from My Heart. This brings up compassion and tears within Terri's eyes and in her Heart. For she knows this space of humbleness. She knows this space of sincerity. And this is where all spiritual students must come to in their Heart Space.

No one outside of you will know, you will recognize it in your Heart. And it will be from a humble Heart that you go before Mother/Father God, for you will recognize that it is only important that you serve. And once you understand how to serve Mother/Father God, then you will recognize the next step is that you serve in JOY!!

This is the space that all Ascension Students will come from. You will learn to serve in a space of Unconditional Love, and from there your JOY will escalate.

I will speak on Unconditional Love in a moment, for I already hear questions within your Heart Space, and I will literally validate this for you in just a moment.

Let us finish the mini-meditation.

From your Heart Space, I want you to use your imagination, this is very important, for the Energy that I create for you now, is how you will create your Light Bodies. You will remember this when the time comes, and you will say, aahh! Sanat showed me this, and you will remember this mini meditation and it will assist you.

From your Heart of Sacred Fire, there is a Cord that moves from your Heart Chakra and it moves up through your throat and it goes all the way up to your 3rd eye.

(NOTE TO READER: Sanat is pointing on Terri from Heart to 3rd eye, a cord running vertically.)

The cord is three-vine, the cord is Nature, Mother God, Father God.

Three vines, running from your Heart to your 3rd Eye. It solidifies in your 3rd eye. This Energy is how you will learn to create your Merkabah, 24/7. You cannot move from your Heart Space until you totally understand Unconditional Love.

I will guide you, call on My Energy. I will explain this to you over, and over, and over. I will remind you of your Divine Blueprint, which is already in your Heart Space.

From here you follow this cord, it is a 3-vine cord, Nature, Mother God, Father God Energy. The cord is Green, and around the cord is Father God, which is Gold, and Mother God, which is Silver. Gold is Masculine, Silver is Feminine and between these two places this cord runs. Now in your 3rd eye there is a Violet Pyramid, it is a Hologram that literally moves in a clockwise position, and this beautiful Violet Pyramid, sits on an Etheric Level right there within and around your 3rd eye. The Violet Pyramid also is in your Heart Space, these Two pyramids literally keep this energy solidified in Mother/Father God Energy.

If you were to step outside of your body, and you were to look back at yourself, on an Etheric Level in your God Presence, you would see these Two Energies moving all the time, all the time. Now there are also, concentric, figure-eight circles, the Alpha and Omega Energy, that start at your feet, it moves all around your body and it moves all the way up to your crown chakra. Now this also is your Light Body Energy, once you are able to get a visual on this, you will be able to learn how to connect with your Merkabah more often.

This is what you are going to be learning to do in the next couple of years. It will be that gift that you give to Mother Earth. The Light Body will be shown to those who have earned the privilege. It is a privilege to be able to move in your Light Body, it is your Eternal

Vehicle. It is a body that does not age, it is a body that is inter-dimensional. You will be able to move through dimensions. You will not know aging, you will not have a want or need, and you will be able to create. I guarantee you; it will not be shown to anyone, until they, first, are able to move from their Heart in Unconditional Love. This is a space of non-judgment!! I am always very aware of the energy, when I present this, that many ask this question, Unconditional Love? It never ceases to amaze Me or the Spiritual Hierarchy how many think that Unconditional Love means they lay down on the ground and they are a rug for their loved ones to walk all over them. Nothing could be farther from the truth!!

Unconditional Love is a space, that you learn to move from and you learn to Qualify Life!!

I will absolutely go into this, in great detail, in My book.

Qualifying Life is the name of the game. I am going to lay that in your laps, and I will expand on this more and more as time goes by. You will hear this again on the recording, and you will think, Sanat you said that? You will forget, and when you hear it again on the recording, the seeds are being planted within you.

(NOTE TO READER: I AM SANAT KUMARA, and each time you read My book you WILL learn something new, and that is Good, that is very Good!)

You are learning how to Qualify Life, this is how you become Master of Your Energy, and it is how you learn to move from a space of Unconditional Love.

Unconditional Love does not mean that anyone walks on you, no one walks on you.

You learn how to create healthy boundaries, and you learn to move from a space of non-judgment. Mother/Father God does not judge, Mother/Father God allows all to express and experience. Mother/Father God does not look at anything as right or wrong, good or bad. That was the ***Illusion*** that you said you would participate in. It has always been the ***Illusion.***

You said you would come back and I said I would come back and remind you of your contract. You signed the contract. It is hard to imagine sometimes, when you are being slapped in the face. It is hard!! You look at yourself, and say why God did I choose this?

Why God, Why?

I assure you, God has the greatest compassion for each one of you. God understands the pain that you have been through. God understands your situations and God loves you.

God loves you more than I can possibly even say through the English language, through Terri's mouth right now. Just take My word for it, when I say to you, how much Mother/Father God loves you.

Mother/Father God honors your presence in this 3D expression. You have much Energy that is here to assist you tonight, and from this day forward, your life will not be the same. I assure you, when you walk out of this room, you take Me with you. I will go with you, I will be with you and in your hour of need, you will call on My Energy, Sanat Kumara, and I will assist you to be able to open that 3rd eye and see through the ***Illusion*** that has held you down.

(NOTE TO READER: Sanat Kumara wants you to understand He will assist those who call upon Him, just ask in the sincerity of your Heart and He will come to you.)

It is the ***Illusion*** that you said you would participate in and we are not going to get into the whys. ***The whys have held mankind up, for centuries, upon centuries!!***

You have spent thousands of lifetimes asking why? Now is the lifetime for you to put the 'why' aside, and say *'thy will be done, Mother/Father God, thy will be done!!'*

This is the lifetime that you have the choice to make. You continue to ask the 'why's' and you will not hear the answers!!

The journey back to that, which created you, is a journey of faith!!

And so, (watch Terri, she will hold her hand up in front of her face) and I AM here to tell you, 99.9% of your journey is in Faith. And you will say to God, I cannot see my hand in front of my face God, and yet my Heart tells me, my hand is there!!!

And so God, thy will be done!! It is a journey of Love and it is a journey of Faith!!

It is a childlike journey, for I tell you now, Mother/Father God asks you to come back with a childlike Heart. You open your Heart up to God as a child would!! A child does not question, a child looks in the eyes of the parent and says, I love you God, guide me.

This is what God wants each one of you to do, and these are those SOULS that will be awarded their Light Bodies. This brings up compassion in Terri, for she has known this journey, she understands this.

Yes, there is sacrifice. You learn to walk away from all attachments. It is an interesting walk, this life on Mother Earth. Buddha, said it, you come to a space of non-attachment.

You learn to let go of all the emotional attachments. You will understand that which emotionally attaches you. You will understand that which you need to learn to let go of.

Call on My Energy, call on the Angelic Realm. Call on your Spirit Guides, and We will assist you to be able to let go of the old paradigm. It has not served your Highest Interests. The old paradigm was the *Illusion.*

How long do you continue to live in the ***Illusion?***

When are you ready to take the step of faith and say, thy will be done Mother/Father God, thy will be done. ***It is a leap of joy.*** For you will leave behind you, that which no longer serves a positive purpose in your life and you will move forward in a manner that will literally take you Light Years into your Light Body.

You have SOUL Group Energy that surrounds each one of you. I need to clarify this.

Each one of you has SOUL Energy; you have come from SOUL Group. Each one of you has come from a CORE of SOUL Group Energy. So within, your particular SOUL Group, there is vast energy. Within each one of you, there is Ascended Energy in each one of your SOUL Groups. Ascended Energy is also there for your benefit.

This is where you start to open up your 3rd eye, you start to be present with your awareness and you start to say, OH, Sanat says I have SOUL Group Energy. I can start pulling from a Collective Consciousness that will assist me to cross my 't's' and dot my 'i's' better, so that I don't have to keep returning to the old stuff.

You know the old stuff; it keeps tripping you up, it keeps giving you problems, daily. You don't have to keep doing that. What you need to do, is become aware of your SOUL Group Energy, it is a vast resource of information for each one of you.

Anything that tells you different is a lie! It is the ***Illusion.*** Anything that robs you of the Love of Mother/Father God Energy is the ***Illusion.*** And yet, you said you would participate in that. You said, I will come back and do the ***Illusion*** one more time!!

This is what you need to ask yourself in the quietness of your Heart? Is this the last one for you? Are you ready to take the final steps, for all spiritual ascension students that they must take? There is much information coming for you this evening.

And I AM literally laying much in your laps tonight and I will not let up on any one of you.

Now that you have walked through My Door, I am here to insure that you will listen to your SOUL Group Energy.

(NOTE TO READER: Sanat wants you to know this all applies to you, also.)

It is the 'I AM' Energy, that is the Signature Key of Mother/Father God. 'I AM'. This is Mother/Father God, and it is only Mother/Father God that gives LIFE. And the only way that you are given LIFE (and it is not about a physical body I AM explaining).

LIFE is given to those that move from their Heart in Unconditional Love, they learn to Master their Energy as they Qualify Life every second. And you learn to Qualify Life with your mouth first, this is where we respect!

All Energy from Mother/Father God is always with respect. This has been a journey for Terri that she has been working on for many years, and she has learned through trial and error, if she cannot respect with her mouth, she was to seal her lips shut and turn the key. She has learned she absolutely must respect with her mouth, and from there, Terri has learned to *respect with her vibration.* She has learned to Honor Mother/Father God in all of Life. She has learned it through trial and error, and now she moves in JOY in this. She understands what respect is.

You must come to a space of respect for all of Life. This is a part of your Ascension process.

You must also learn to take responsibility for everything that you do. Whether it is a thought that you are thinking, it is something that you are saying, or an action that you are taking. You are learning to take responsibility for your Energy. And this is becoming Master of Your Energy.

It becomes difficult at times, it becomes difficult.

Abraham has delivered greatness upon your Earth. Abraham, coming through Jerry and Esther Hicks. Abraham has delivered much, much, much wonderful Energy!

And so I AM choosing to take it one step further, I will be presenting the Spiritual Aspect of the Law of Attraction. It is not for everyone. There will be those that say this is too hard for me, I cannot do this, and that is OK. That is OK, another time, another place. They will have a different journey, and they will have other opportunities.

I assure you, ALL will return to that which created them. And eventually, when those return to that which created them, they will have to look within their Heart of Sacred Fire, and they will understand whether they got the lesson or not. It is their journey.

So you will learn that moving from your Heart is an interesting Energy, and you will always learn to remember that there is an Energy here, (Terri points between Heart and 3rd Eye Chakras) and you notice, I have brought Nature into this.

Nature is very much a part of your Ascension Process. Kuthumi is very much a part of this. Nature is what brings everything into manifestation. Without Nature you would have nothing on your Planet. It is Nature that brings it all into manifestation for you to enjoy. So you have much to thank Nature for!!

(NOTE TO READER: SK wants All to understand, Nature only knows the Will of Mother/Father God, and so Nature is responsible for that which is manifested that vibrates the Will of God. That which does not vibrate the Will of God, is not of Love and Light and therefore is not from Nature.)

The Angelic Realm is right here working with everyone on the Ascension Process. It is absolutely a part of the plan that Mother/Father God has created on your Planet. So it is Nature, Angels and Spiritual Hierarchy that are working with you.

It is up to you to decide if you want to go there with these Spiritual Ascension Keys.

I am going to allow questions now:

HARRIET: I am interested in some ways we can be Master of Our Energy, things that we can do, I know I am working on that and are there some things I can do that would be helpful?

SK: Thank You Precious Harriet for coming this evening. Very good question. How does one Qualify Life?

One learns as they become present with their awareness on a daily basis. ***They begin to recognize that they can Qualify Life with their mouth!***

Terri is very much, picking up on My Energy, throughout her day, if she is in a conversation with people, and she recognizes that the vibration that might come through her mouth is not life giving. Now here, I AM going to underline **LIFE-Giving.** If there is a statement that she is going to be making, or if the train of thought coming from her mouth is not going to be life-supporting, joy filled and life-giving, she recognizes that she needs to keep her mouth shut. She understands that the things she says need to be life-supporting and life-giving. And Terri is finding, she is wasting her Energy if she is not ***giving life.*** She understands this, recognizing it more and more. I have been observing Terri and as I observe, I notice a Peace in Terri that she did not have a year ago.

(NOTE TO READER: This is Terri, and I would like to share with you the reader, Sanat Kumara has wonderfully assisted me in understanding and executing Qualifying Life, and as a direct result the Peace and Joy that fill my daily life are amazing.)

She understands that as she **expresses her God-Presence daily, by Qualifying Life with her mouth, she recognizes that the Peace grows in her Heart. And she is finding that her needs are becoming less and less. It is a feeling that you find, the more you move in this Space of Qualifying Life with your Vibration, Qualifying Life with your mouth, you recognize that your needs become less and less. God is moving in you more and more. It is a beautiful place to move from. And it IS a place of evolving. It is a place of En-Light-en-ment. It is a place of Love and Light.**

Please do call on My Energy; I would love to share this with you. One recognizes as they move through their day, you will be able to **Honor Life;** you will be able to **Respect Life. And you find that it comes with your conversation and with your vibration. So there is a present awareness there.**

I want to assure you, if you find yourself thinking the words **'be careful'** please don't do that. This puts you in a vibration of 'stuck', I am walking on egg-shells, Oh My!!

That is not what Mother/Father God wants you to do.

Mother/Father God wants you to be Present, have an awareness of Qualifying Life with your mouth, with your vibration, with your thoughts. So this is taking on more of a Spiritual Aspect. And as you learn to Qualify Life, and I will show you how, it will give you a Peace and Joy in your Heart that nothing else will ever touch.

You will find that your life will lay in front of you and

it will be so evolved and it will be so beautiful, you will think Oh My, I really don't have many needs anymore. Your needs will become less and less and the World will open up to you in a manner that only God can do for you.

So this is awareness, learning to Qualify Life. I assure you, Qualified Energy is LIFE.

(Mis)-Qualified Energy is DEATH. And you will know, when you have (Mis)-Qualified Energy, for it will leave you feeling less-than. Qualified Energy is Life. (Mis)-Qualified Energy is Death. And you will know, (mis)-qualified energy will leave you feeling empty.

Qualifying Life will leave you feeling Peaceful and Joy-filled. There is the difference and you will learn.

This has been a part of everyone's journey, walking through the ILLUSION. All Spiritual Students must learn, they are either Master of their Energy or Energy is Master of them. You will come to this recognition and you must absolutely learn how to Master your Energy by Qualifying Life!!

And it starts and stops with the Violet Light.

So, I AM going to bring in Master Saint Germaine now. Harriet, close your eyes, this is going to benefit the group and I will direct this towards Harriet because she has asked, and this is for Group Energy.

Saint Germaine has stepped in now in front of you, He is opening your Heart Chakra now with the Violet Light and We are enmeshing your Heart Chakra now with the Violet Light. You are going to be feeling a warmth within your Heart Chakra that you have not felt before. ***This is the Violet Light. We are going to be transmuting old energies that no longer serve a positive purpose within your life.***

The Violet Light is the Holy Spirit; it brings

Mother/Father God Energy on Mother Earth.

Imagine now the Violet Light in your Heart Space and it will assist you in Qualifying old negative energy that is no longer useful in your life. (Another tool in Qualifying Life)

Remember, I do not know time or space. So I can be in several areas all at the same time.

Your 3rd eye will be opened in a manner that it has never been opened before and We will bring in your SOUL Group Energy that are going to be pulling for you.

It is time for you to take the next grand leap in your spiritual consciousness and you are right Harriet, you are a Light Worker on Mother Earth. You have much SOUL Group Energy to pull from. There is the most beautiful Violet Pyramid in your Heart Space. You are getting ready to understand your Cosmic Beingness, and I have been waiting to share this with you.

FLOR: And you have spoken so beautiful about everything. I find my energy comes and goes. And I am off track. And I want to find my passion. And I have the energy and then it is gone. I need guidance.

SK: I thank you for sharing what you have just shared. As I look at you, I see flowers all around you, such beautiful flowers. You have come in with much beauty Flor, and you have yet to express the Spiritual Beauty that you have within you for, this is coming. I want to assure you Mother Mary is one of your main spirit guides, She is standing behind you. And She is stepping in now for you, as I stand in front of you.

Mother Mary is literally throwing her roses all over your physical body, and She is wanting to share with you, if you will open up to Mother Mary, she will help you heal old wounds. There are old wounds in your Heart Space that need healing.

You have all come in this evening with the energy of '7', which are your spiritual lessons. Each one of you has spiritual lessons that you are literally closing up. So you are at the end of your spiritual lessons. Some of you are still have more steps to take in the next couple of years. Some of you are literally solidifying, and you recognize that the old spiritual lessons are over. This is very good. The Energy in here is so ripe.

Flor it is Mother Mary that will assist you to be able to heal old Heart wounds. You are not quite ready yet for Me to solidify this for you. Please do not be disappointed; listen to what it is I have to share with you.

You need to work this through in the sleep state, you will know when this is done for you, for when it is, you will wake up with a Peacefulness that you never had before.

Mother Mary and Myself will be working with you in the sleep state. You are not in your physical body in the sleep state at night. This is why many of you wake up very tired in the morning, you are not in your physical bodies, you all journey. You journey in your Cosmic Beingness; you are by far grander than your physical bodies. This is very good!!

With SOUL Group, with Mother/Father God, with your Spirit Guides, with Myself and Beloved Mother Mary, we have much to do in the sleep state.

After 7 days time, you will wake up with a peace in your Heart, that you have never had before, including this one.

Your passion, Flor, you are a multi-talented lady. You have been given a wealth of value from your Heart Space to be able to help people to see within themselves. You have the ability to sit and talk with a person, and help them to do introspection.

This is a gift you have already been given, once

your Heart has been healed from those old energies, and you have that Peace in your Heart, then, I want you to call on My Energy and Mother Mary's, and We will guide you as how to proceed to fulfill your destiny. You have the ability to assist people to do a beautiful introspection. This needs to be taken from a Spiritual Vantage Point. We will guide you, you will be saying guide me God, I am ready to fulfill my destiny with my passion and guide me God, guide, me, thy will be done God in my life, thy will be done.

You will recognize that your life will take volumes in Light Years, and you will recognize that you are going to approach your career from a different vantage point that you were never able to do before. I will be working with your SOUL Group Energy.

Mother Mary is the Twin Flame of Archangel Raphael, They work with the Heart Chakra.

Mother Mary, her Signature is the Blue Diamond Sapphire, so when you are aware of that, or the Roses, or the Emerald Green Light, you are aware of Mother Mary.

LINDA: You spoke of Unconditional Love and not being a door mat, and not letting people walk on you. Can you expand on that, and how people who want to work in Unconditional Love, being on this negative Earth, it is very, very hard.

SK: I thank you for sharing your Energy here this evening. I understand this is a big step for you, and I recognize you are moving from a place of great compassion in your Heart.

As I look at you, I see such love in your Heart, and such a willingness to help others.

It is absolutely admirable, and yet, I also recognize, it has been for you a double-edged sword. In your eagerness, in your absolute compassion, to help others and it has been from a space of such un-selfishness, you have negated your God Presence.

Somehow, along the way, you've forgotten the Joy that is there in your Heart. And it is understandable, for you have immersed yourself in a situation, where people literally are draining you. People daily are robbing you; they are pulling from you, your Energy.

It is very apparent as I look at you, and I say this with the utmost Respect for you. I understand this is how you make your living.

I would like to assist you greatly, and what I Am going to encourage you to do, from this day forward, call My Energy into your Life daily, so that I may help your Heart open up and recognize that God is greater in you than that which you see in the world.

I understand that you see the negativity, I understand. I see that the possibility for you to move down a beautiful new path is there for you, and yet, as I look at you, I recognize first, your Heart must heal. This is not your fault on a conscious level, this is ingrained in you, and it is what you came in with. That is alright.

I would like to work with you, if you will allow Me. If you will call on My energy, and listen to this recording, you will be able to say, maybe I can look beyond what I see daily, maybe I need somehow to call on Sanat to heal my Heart. For your Heart is heavy, I look at you with great compassion and great respect. Your work ethics are admirable; no one can take that away from you. And yet it is the very thing that has become the double-edged sword for you. So with that, I would share with you, that there is another avenue for you, and yet, before this other avenue is able to open for you, it is your Heart that must be healed, and **I AM in the Heart business!!!**

If you will please allow Me to work with you in the sleep state, ask Me, to please come into your life and work with you. I always move in Peach Energy. And I only know LOVE, so when I come to you, you will feel great LOVE in your Heart and great Peacefulness, for this is who I AM. And I will bring Mother/Father God Energy to you, so that you are able to open up and allow your Heart Space to heal. ***And allow the Unconditional Love of Mother/Father God to heal your Heart Space.***

(NOTE TO READER: Sanat wants you to know, if this information speaks to you, He will come, if you call and assist in the Healing of your Heart Space)

JOANNA: The first thought Sanat, I am so thankful you came into my life, and I don't know how to thank you for your help in the past couple of months, it was a great help and I was very happy you helped me and I know it is you! I feel there is an exploding inside of energy and joy and charisma, and how can I convert it to a physical world? I have this tremendous energy, but I focus on small stuff, I think I have Attention Deficit Disorder, and I feel that I cannot move forward with my achievements. I know there is something I have to create, a company, an organization or a masterpiece. But there is something that stops me and I would like to know how to remove it.

SK: I thank you Joanna, and I thank you for your energy here this evening. And as I look at you, I agree, you have much beautiful energy within you, much to share on Mother Earth. And you are right; you have a passion yet to unfold. And you will create a masterpiece. As I look at you, I assure you, if you will start to use the Violet Light, as I have directed all of you in this circle, it will assist you, to be able to control the Energies that scatter you.

(NOTE TO READER: Sanat pointed with Terri's hands out away from her physical body.) When you find you're out here, you need to come back to your Heart Space, and you need to say ***Guide Me God,***

Guide Me, Thy Will Be Done, Thy Will Be Done.

Recognize you are out here, and come back to your Heart, and say Guide Me God, Guide Me.

See the Violet Light in all Seven of your Major Chakras and this will solidify the scattered energies and bring them back to the present moment. And you will learn to move from your Heart of Sacred Fire!!

It is not time yet, Joanna for you to gift mankind with that of your Spiritual Energy. It is not time yet for you. You will know when the time is right, for the door will open, that was not there before. And you will sit down on your rear end and you will say "Good Grief, where did that door come from, it wasn't there before!!"

Because you were not ready Joanna!! When you are ready, the door will open, and you will be so focused, you will be so present, and you will be so ready to manifest the Will of Mother/Father God.

You are being prepared for this, call on My Energy and I will assist you. You need to get in the mood and the momentum and the swing of Energy of creating God's Will in your Life. This is a space of submission, it is a space of surrender, it is a space of sincerity, and it is a space of humbleness, and finally, it is a space of joy.

And you use the Violet Light to get you there. The Violet Light will solidify all this Energy that is scattering you and you will learn to move from that Heart Space. So stay tuned, Joanna, I will keep working with you!

And once again, I want to share this with you before I leave. I still stand on what I originally told you, if you can come to a place of learning to do some volunteer work, this will help you solidify some old energies that need to be healed within you.

I am not going to tell you which way to go, as I look at you, from My Perspective, I would give you My suggestion of looking into an avenue of volunteering with children.

Now as I speak this to you, I hear the questions raised in your mind.

I am not telling you what to do, I do not do this. I will not tell you what to do, I am only sharing with you Joanna, that if you are able to come to a place, where you can move from a volunteering standpoint, you will find that some old energies in your Heart will be laid to rest. And you will be able to bring peace into your life that you were not able to do before. And this will be solidified through the volunteering avenue.

If you will call on Me and be open, I will guide you. I will guide you; always I bring the Will of Mother/Father God. I only do that which is for the Highest Good of the individual. So if you are ready to take that road, open your Heart and allow Me to guide you, and I will show you that path. And from there you will find another door will open for you down the road, and it will be The Door that you will share your passion on this Planet. You are not ready to open that door yet, for there are still some lessons that have to be solidified for you. I share this with you in Joy. I must bring this to a close.

As you listen to the CD, your questions will be answered on an Intuitive level.

(NOTE TO THE READER: I AM SANAT KUMARA, and as you read this, if it speaks to your Heart, I will assist you, call on My Ascended Peach Energy.)

Call on My Energy and I will assist you to be able to cross your 't's' and dot your 'i's.

I AM Sanat Kumara.

SANAT KUMARA'S MANTRAS
FOR ASCENSION DIMENSION

1. I AM THAT I AM

2. I AM PERFECT REGENERATION DIAMOND
   CORE GOD CELL

3. I AM VIBRATING CAUSAL BODY HIGHEST GOOD

4. I AM DIVINE INTENTION, GOD'S WILL FULFILLS
   ALL MY DESIRES

5. I AM DIVINE INTENTION, ALIGN WITH CAUSAL
   BODY & BE, I AM.

6. I AM ASCENDED AND FREE

7. I AM MANIFESTING GOD'S WILL IN JOY

8. I AM SACRED FIRE, I AM SACRED FIRE,
   I AM SACRED FIRE

9. (Memorize My Sacred Fire poem, and your day
   will escalate in JOY)

DEFINITIONS OF TERMS

Ascension Dimension: The ability to move into your Freedom, from all that does not serve a positive purpose

Divine Intention: Directly connecting with Divine Mind, with Divine Vibration

Divine Mind: Mother/Father God

Divine Vibration: Mother/Father God Energy

Entities: Sanat Kumara uses this expression interchangeably with our physical presence and those who are in the Etheric realm.

Evil: Absence of LIFE

Mother/Father God: That which created us, embracing Yin and Yang, Negative and Positive, Female and Male Energies, I AM

Divine Parents: Mother/Father God

I AM: Your Monad, your God Presence, the Signature Energy of Mother/Father God

LIFE: THE avenue to expand Divine Mind through Divine Vibration and the perfect blending of LOVE AND LIGHT, AKA Abundant Life.

About the Author

Terri Love

Terri has been a serious student of spiritual wisdom in the metaphysical realm for over 35 years. Terri is an Ordained Minister, Certified Hypnotherapist, and Jin Shin Jyutsu Practitioner, in the Phoenix Metropolitan Area. This Master Teacher of Spiritual Awareness has combined an eclectic mixture of Holistic Modalities, with the Emotional Freedom Technique. She empowers body, mind, and spirit, through classes, private sessions and phone conferences.

College students have enjoyed Terri's Meditation and Past Life Regression classes. She enjoys sharing her energy and enthusiasm through public speaking and group workshops to facilitate Innate Wisdom for Spiritual Healing and Empowerment on All levels.

She has taught J.A.O.G.I. (Joy Awareness of Guided Imagery) in group workshops, including The Southern Arizona Summit, working with the Courts for Arizona's Foster Children.

Terri creates custom tapes for her clients to listen to daily, allowing the Angelic Realm to work through the vibration of her voice.

The Great White Brotherhood of Ascended Masters, Royal Angelic Realm and Nature Family have blessed Terri's ability to minister the Highest Good of her clients. In January of 2006, Beloved Ascended Master Sanat Kumara lovingly entered her life and now you are reading His Teachings as Dialoged through Terri, published by Ancient Wisdom Publishing.

For more information visit www.terrilove.com.